C-1068 CAREER EXAMINATION SERIES

This is your
PASSBOOK for...

Train Operator

Test Preparation Study Guide
Questions & Answers

NATIONAL LEARNING CORPORATION®

COPYRIGHT NOTICE

This book is SOLELY intended for, is sold ONLY to, and its use is RESTRICTED to individual, bona fide applicants or candidates who qualify by virtue of having seriously filed applications for appropriate license, certificate, professional and/or promotional advancement, higher school matriculation, scholarship, or other legitimate requirements of education and/or governmental authorities.

This book is NOT intended for use, class instruction, tutoring, training, duplication, copying, reprinting, excerption, or adaptation, etc., by:

1) Other publishers
2) Proprietors and/or Instructors of "Coaching" and/or Preparatory Courses
3) Personnel and/or Training Divisions of commercial, industrial, and governmental organizations
4) Schools, colleges, or universities and/or their departments and staffs, including teachers and other personnel
5) Testing Agencies or Bureaus
6) Study groups which seek by the purchase of a single volume to copy and/or duplicate and/or adapt this material for use by the group as a whole without having purchased individual volumes for each of the members of the group
7) Et al.

Such persons would be in violation of appropriate Federal and State statutes.

PROVISION OF LICENSING AGREEMENTS – Recognized educational, commercial, industrial, and governmental institutions and organizations, and others legitimately engaged in educational pursuits, including training, testing, and measurement activities, may address request for a licensing agreement to the copyright owners, who will determine whether, and under what conditions, including fees and charges, the materials in this book may be used them. In other words, a licensing facility exists for the legitimate use of the material in this book on other than an individual basis. However, it is asseverated and affirmed here that the material in this book CANNOT be used without the receipt of the express permission of such a licensing agreement from the Publishers. Inquiries re licensing should be addressed to the company, attention rights and permissions department.

All rights reserved, including the right of reproduction in whole or in part, in any form or by any means, electronic or mechanical, including photocopying, recording, or by any information storage and retrieval system, without permission in writing from the Publisher.

Copyright © 2024 by
National Learning Corporation

212 Michael Drive, Syosset, NY 11791
(516) 921-8888 • www.passbooks.com
E-mail: info@passbooks.com

PUBLISHED IN THE UNITED STATES OF AMERICA

PASSBOOK® SERIES

THE *PASSBOOK® SERIES* has been created to prepare applicants and candidates for the ultimate academic battlefield – the examination room.

At some time in our lives, each and every one of us may be required to take an examination – for validation, matriculation, admission, qualification, registration, certification, or licensure.

Based on the assumption that every applicant or candidate has met the basic formal educational standards, has taken the required number of courses, and read the necessary texts, the *PASSBOOK® SERIES* furnishes the one special preparation which may assure passing with confidence, instead of failing with insecurity. Examination questions – together with answers – are furnished as the basic vehicle for study so that the mysteries of the examination and its compounding difficulties may be eliminated or diminished by a sure method.

This book is meant to help you pass your examination provided that you qualify and are serious in your objective.

The entire field is reviewed through the huge store of content information which is succinctly presented through a provocative and challenging approach – the question-and-answer method.

A climate of success is established by furnishing the correct answers at the end of each test.

You soon learn to recognize types of questions, forms of questions, and patterns of questioning. You may even begin to anticipate expected outcomes.

You perceive that many questions are repeated or adapted so that you can gain acute insights, which may enable you to score many sure points.

You learn how to confront new questions, or types of questions, and to attack them confidently and work out the correct answers.

You note objectives and emphases, and recognize pitfalls and dangers, so that you may make positive educational adjustments.

Moreover, you are kept fully informed in relation to new concepts, methods, practices, and directions in the field.

You discover that you are actually taking the examination all the time: you are preparing for the examination by "taking" an examination, not by reading extraneous and/or supererogatory textbooks.

In short, this PASSBOOK®, used directedly, should be an important factor in helping you to pass your test.

TRAIN OPERATOR

DUTIES AND RESPONSIBILITIES

Train Operators, under supervision, have direct responsibility for the safe, timely and proper operation of New York City Transit Authority multi-unit subway cars, subway service cars and trains in accordance with the rules, regulations and special instructions governing such operation. They operate trains in revenue and non-revenue road service, and in yard or terminal service; prepare trains for road service and switch cars in yards; in revenue road service, convey passengers over assigned routes; may open and close doors in stations and terminals; may make announcements; in non-revenue road service, operate work trains and revenue collection trains; in yards and terminal service, switch cars, prepare trains for road service and operate trains between yards and terminals; convey trains into barns and shops for inspection and repair, and through car washes for cleaning; wear a prescribed uniform; and perform related work.

Some of the physical activities performed by Train Operators and environmental conditions experienced are: climbing and descending ladders on and off the tracks, ascending and descending from trains and catwalks to roadbeds; walking along elevated sections of track; responding to audible signals such as alarm bells, train whistles, horns and radio conversation; responding to visual signals including distinguishing colored lights; using manual equipment related to train operation; remaining in a sitting position for extended periods of time; and lifting heavy equipment.

SCOPE OF THE EXAMINATION

The multiple-choice test may include questions on understanding and applying written material relating to the rules, regulations and operating procedures governing safe and efficient train operation; ability to read and understand written material on train controls, car equipment and railroad signals; ability to apply appropriate procedures in emergency or stressful situations; understanding military time; and other abilities including:

Written Comprehension — The ability to understand written sentences or paragraphs. Example: Understanding written bulletins released by Transit.
Written Expression — The ability to use English words or sentences in writing so others will understand. Example: Writing incident reports regarding unusual occurrences.
Problem Sensitivity — The ability to tell when something is wrong or likely to go wrong. It includes being able to identify the whole problem as well as elements of the problem. Example: Recognizing that an object on the track may interfere with the normal operation of the train.
Deductive Reasoning — The ability to apply general rules to specific problems to come up with logical answers. It involves deciding if an answer makes sense. Example: Applying Transit rules and regulations to situations to determine the appropriate action that must be taken.
Inductive Reasoning — The ability to combine separate pieces of information, or specific answers to problems to form general rules or conclusions. It includes coming up with a logical explanation for why a series of unrelated events occur together. Example: Determining the action that must be taken based on a combination of observations on the tracks and radio chatter from other train operators, the Rail Control Center or maintainers performing repairs along the trackway.
Information Ordering — The ability to follow correctly a rule or set of rules to arrange things or actions in a certain order. The rule or sets of rules used must be given. The things or actions to be put in order can include numbers, letters, words, pictures, procedures, sentences, and mathematical or logical operations. Example: Following a step-by-step procedure to connect a cable to the third rail for power.
Spatial Orientation — The ability to tell where you are in relation to the location of some object or to tell where the object is in relation to you. Example: Reading a schematic diagram to determine track configurations.
Number Facility — The ability involving the degree to which adding, subtracting, multiplying, and dividing can be done quickly and correctly. Example: Performing mathematical calculations using track markers to determine the current location. Mathematics Reasoning — The ability to understand and organize a problem and then to select a mathematical method or formula to solve the problem. Example: Determining the mathematics required to calculate distances between track markings.
Mechanical Aptitude — The ability to understand and apply mechanical concepts and principles to solve problems. Example: Understanding how a train's brake pressure affects its ability to brake.
Visualization — The ability to imagine how something will look after it is moved around or when its parts are moved or rearranged. Example: Imagining how a track configuration changes after a switch moves it.

HOW TO TAKE A TEST

I. YOU MUST PASS AN EXAMINATION

A. WHAT EVERY CANDIDATE SHOULD KNOW

Examination applicants often ask us for help in preparing for the written test. What can I study in advance? What kinds of questions will be asked? How will the test be given? How will the papers be graded?

As an applicant for a civil service examination, you may be wondering about some of these things. Our purpose here is to suggest effective methods of advance study and to describe civil service examinations.

Your chances for success on this examination can be increased if you know how to prepare. Those "pre-examination jitters" can be reduced if you know what to expect. You can even experience an adventure in good citizenship if you know why civil service exams are given.

B. WHY ARE CIVIL SERVICE EXAMINATIONS GIVEN?

Civil service examinations are important to you in two ways. As a citizen, you want public jobs filled by employees who know how to do their work. As a job seeker, you want a fair chance to compete for that job on an equal footing with other candidates. The best-known means of accomplishing this two-fold goal is the competitive examination.

Exams are widely publicized throughout the nation. They may be administered for jobs in federal, state, city, municipal, town or village governments or agencies.

Any citizen may apply, with some limitations, such as the age or residence of applicants. Your experience and education may be reviewed to see whether you meet the requirements for the particular examination. When these requirements exist, they are reasonable and applied consistently to all applicants. Thus, a competitive examination may cause you some uneasiness now, but it is your privilege and safeguard.

C. HOW ARE CIVIL SERVICE EXAMS DEVELOPED?

Examinations are carefully written by trained technicians who are specialists in the field known as "psychological measurement," in consultation with recognized authorities in the field of work that the test will cover. These experts recommend the subject matter areas or skills to be tested; only those knowledges or skills important to your success on the job are included. The most reliable books and source materials available are used as references. Together, the experts and technicians judge the difficulty level of the questions.

Test technicians know how to phrase questions so that the problem is clearly stated. Their ethics do not permit "trick" or "catch" questions. Questions may have been tried out on sample groups, or subjected to statistical analysis, to determine their usefulness.

Written tests are often used in combination with performance tests, ratings of training and experience, and oral interviews. All of these measures combine to form the best-known means of finding the right person for the right job.

II. HOW TO PASS THE WRITTEN TEST

A. NATURE OF THE EXAMINATION

To prepare intelligently for civil service examinations, you should know how they differ from school examinations you have taken. In school you were assigned certain definite pages to read or subjects to cover. The examination questions were quite detailed and usually emphasized memory. Civil service exams, on the other hand, try to discover your present ability to perform the duties of a position, plus your potentiality to learn these duties. In other words, a civil service exam attempts to predict how successful you will be. Questions cover such a broad area that they cannot be as minute and detailed as school exam questions.

In the public service similar kinds of work, or positions, are grouped together in one "class." This process is known as *position-classification*. All the positions in a class are paid according to the salary range for that class. One class title covers all of these positions, and they are all tested by the same examination.

B. FOUR BASIC STEPS

1) Study the announcement

How, then, can you know what subjects to study? Our best answer is: "Learn as much as possible about the class of positions for which you've applied." The exam will test the knowledge, skills and abilities needed to do the work.

Your most valuable source of information about the position you want is the official exam announcement. This announcement lists the training and experience qualifications. Check these standards and apply only if you come reasonably close to meeting them.

The brief description of the position in the examination announcement offers some clues to the subjects which will be tested. Think about the job itself. Review the duties in your mind. Can you perform them, or are there some in which you are rusty? Fill in the blank spots in your preparation.

Many jurisdictions preview the written test in the exam announcement by including a section called "Knowledge and Abilities Required," "Scope of the Examination," or some similar heading. Here you will find out specifically what fields will be tested.

2) Review your own background

Once you learn in general what the position is all about, and what you need to know to do the work, ask yourself which subjects you already know fairly well and which need improvement. You may wonder whether to concentrate on improving your strong areas or on building some background in your fields of weakness. When the announcement has specified "some knowledge" or "considerable knowledge," or has used adjectives like "beginning principles of..." or "advanced ... methods," you can get a clue as to the number and difficulty of questions to be asked in any given field. More questions, and hence broader coverage, would be included for those subjects which are more important in the work. Now weigh your strengths and weaknesses against the job requirements and prepare accordingly.

3) Determine the level of the position

Another way to tell how intensively you should prepare is to understand the level of the job for which you are applying. Is it the entering level? In other words, is this the position in which beginners in a field of work are hired? Or is it an intermediate or advanced level? Sometimes this is indicated by such words as "Junior" or "Senior" in the class title. Other jurisdictions use Roman numerals to designate the level – Clerk I, Clerk II, for example. The word "Supervisor" sometimes appears in the title. If the level is not indicated by the title, check the description of duties. Will you be working under very close supervision, or will you have responsibility for independent decisions in this work?

4) Choose appropriate study materials

Now that you know the subjects to be examined and the relative amount of each subject to be covered, you can choose suitable study materials. For beginning level jobs, or even advanced ones, if you have a pronounced weakness in some aspect of your training, read a modern, standard textbook in that field. Be sure it is up to date and has general coverage. Such books are normally available at your library, and the librarian will be glad to help you locate one. For entry-level positions, questions of appropriate difficulty are chosen – neither highly advanced questions, nor those too simple. Such questions require careful thought but not advanced training.

If the position for which you are applying is technical or advanced, you will read more advanced, specialized material. If you are already familiar with the basic principles of your field, elementary textbooks would waste your time. Concentrate on advanced textbooks and technical periodicals. Think through the concepts and review difficult problems in your field.

These are all general sources. You can get more ideas on your own initiative, following these leads. For example, training manuals and publications of the government agency which employs workers in your field can be useful, particularly for technical and professional positions. A letter or visit to the government department involved may result in more specific study suggestions, and certainly will provide you with a more definite idea of the exact nature of the position you are seeking.

III. KINDS OF TESTS

Tests are used for purposes other than measuring knowledge and ability to perform specified duties. For some positions, it is equally important to test ability to make adjustments to new situations or to profit from training. In others, basic mental abilities not dependent on information are essential. Questions which test these things may not appear as pertinent to the duties of the position as those which test for knowledge and information. Yet they are often highly important parts of a fair examination. For very general questions, it is almost impossible to help you direct your study efforts. What we can do is to point out some of the more common of these general abilities needed in public service positions and describe some typical questions.

1) General information

Broad, general information has been found useful for predicting job success in some kinds of work. This is tested in a variety of ways, from vocabulary lists to questions about current events. Basic background in some field of work, such as sociology or economics, may be sampled in a group of questions. Often these are principles which have become familiar to most persons through exposure rather than through formal training. It is difficult to advise you how to study for these questions; being alert to the world around you is our best suggestion.

2) Verbal ability

An example of an ability needed in many positions is verbal or language ability. Verbal ability is, in brief, the ability to use and understand words. Vocabulary and grammar tests are typical measures of this ability. Reading comprehension or paragraph interpretation questions are common in many kinds of civil service tests. You are given a paragraph of written material and asked to find its central meaning.

3) Numerical ability

Number skills can be tested by the familiar arithmetic problem, by checking paired lists of numbers to see which are alike and which are different, or by interpreting charts and graphs. In the latter test, a graph may be printed in the test booklet which you are asked to use as the basis for answering questions.

4) Observation

A popular test for law-enforcement positions is the observation test. A picture is shown to you for several minutes, then taken away. Questions about the picture test your ability to observe both details and larger elements.

5) Following directions

In many positions in the public service, the employee must be able to carry out written instructions dependably and accurately. You may be given a chart with several columns, each column listing a variety of information. The questions require you to carry out directions involving the information given in the chart.

6) Skills and aptitudes

Performance tests effectively measure some manual skills and aptitudes. When the skill is one in which you are trained, such as typing or shorthand, you can practice. These tests are often very much like those given in business school or high school courses. For many of the other skills and aptitudes, however, no short-time preparation can be made. Skills and abilities natural to you or that you have developed throughout your lifetime are being tested.

Many of the general questions just described provide all the data needed to answer the questions and ask you to use your reasoning ability to find the answers. Your best preparation for these tests, as well as for tests of facts and ideas, is to be at your physical and mental best. You, no doubt, have your own methods of getting into an exam-taking mood and keeping "in shape." The next section lists some ideas on this subject.

IV. KINDS OF QUESTIONS

Only rarely is the "essay" question, which you answer in narrative form, used in civil service tests. Civil service tests are usually of the short-answer type. Full instructions for answering these questions will be given to you at the examination. But in case this is your first experience with short-answer questions and separate answer sheets, here is what you need to know:

1) Multiple-choice Questions

Most popular of the short-answer questions is the "multiple choice" or "best answer" question. It can be used, for example, to test for factual knowledge, ability to solve problems or judgment in meeting situations found at work.

A multiple-choice question is normally one of three types—
- It can begin with an incomplete statement followed by several possible endings. You are to find the one ending which *best* completes the statement, although some of the others may not be entirely wrong.
- It can also be a complete statement in the form of a question which is answered by choosing one of the statements listed.

- It can be in the form of a problem – again you select the best answer.

Here is an example of a multiple-choice question with a discussion which should give you some clues as to the method for choosing the right answer:

When an employee has a complaint about his assignment, the action which will *best* help him overcome his difficulty is to
- A. discuss his difficulty with his coworkers
- B. take the problem to the head of the organization
- C. take the problem to the person who gave him the assignment
- D. say nothing to anyone about his complaint

In answering this question, you should study each of the choices to find which is best. Consider choice "A" – Certainly an employee may discuss his complaint with fellow employees, but no change or improvement can result, and the complaint remains unresolved. Choice "B" is a poor choice since the head of the organization probably does not know what assignment you have been given, and taking your problem to him is known as "going over the head" of the supervisor. The supervisor, or person who made the assignment, is the person who can clarify it or correct any injustice. Choice "C" is, therefore, correct. To say nothing, as in choice "D," is unwise. Supervisors have and interest in knowing the problems employees are facing, and the employee is seeking a solution to his problem.

2) True/False Questions

The "true/false" or "right/wrong" form of question is sometimes used. Here a complete statement is given. Your job is to decide whether the statement is right or wrong.

SAMPLE: A roaming cell-phone call to a nearby city costs less than a non-roaming call to a distant city.

This statement is wrong, or false, since roaming calls are more expensive.

This is not a complete list of all possible question forms, although most of the others are variations of these common types. You will always get complete directions for answering questions. Be sure you understand *how* to mark your answers – ask questions until you do.

V. RECORDING YOUR ANSWERS

Computer terminals are used more and more today for many different kinds of exams.

For an examination with very few applicants, you may be told to record your answers in the test booklet itself. Separate answer sheets are much more common. If this separate answer sheet is to be scored by machine – and this is often the case – it is highly important that you mark your answers correctly in order to get credit.

An electronic scoring machine is often used in civil service offices because of the speed with which papers can be scored. Machine-scored answer sheets must be marked with a pencil, which will be given to you. This pencil has a high graphite content which responds to the electronic scoring machine. As a matter of fact, stray dots may register as answers, so do not let your pencil rest on the answer sheet while you are pondering the correct answer. Also, if your pencil lead breaks or is otherwise defective, ask for another.

Since the answer sheet will be dropped in a slot in the scoring machine, be careful not to bend the corners or get the paper crumpled.

The answer sheet normally has five vertical columns of numbers, with 30 numbers to a column. These numbers correspond to the question numbers in your test booklet. After each number, going across the page are four or five pairs of dotted lines. These short dotted lines have small letters or numbers above them. The first two pairs may also have a "T" or "F" above the letters. This indicates that the first two pairs only are to be used if the questions are of the true-false type. If the questions are multiple choice, disregard the "T" and "F" and pay attention only to the small letters or numbers.

Answer your questions in the manner of the sample that follows:

32. The largest city in the United States is
    A. Washington, D.C.
    B. New York City
    C. Chicago
    D. Detroit
    E. San Francisco

1) Choose the answer you think is best. (New York City is the largest, so "B" is correct.)
2) Find the row of dotted lines numbered the same as the question you are answering. (Find row number 32)
3) Find the pair of dotted lines corresponding to the answer. (Find the pair of lines under the mark "B.")
4) Make a solid black mark between the dotted lines.

VI. BEFORE THE TEST

Common sense will help you find procedures to follow to get ready for an examination. Too many of us, however, overlook these sensible measures. Indeed, nervousness and fatigue have been found to be the most serious reasons why applicants fail to do their best on civil service tests. Here is a list of reminders:

- Begin your preparation early – Don't wait until the last minute to go scurrying around for books and materials or to find out what the position is all about.
- Prepare continuously – An hour a night for a week is better than an all-night cram session. This has been definitely established. What is more, a night a week for a month will return better dividends than crowding your study into a shorter period of time.
- Locate the place of the exam – You have been sent a notice telling you when and where to report for the examination. If the location is in a different town or otherwise unfamiliar to you, it would be well to inquire the best route and learn something about the building.
- Relax the night before the test – Allow your mind to rest. Do not study at all that night. Plan some mild recreation or diversion; then go to bed early and get a good night's sleep.
- Get up early enough to make a leisurely trip to the place for the test – This way unforeseen events, traffic snarls, unfamiliar buildings, etc. will not upset you.
- Dress comfortably – A written test is not a fashion show. You will be known by number and not by name, so wear something comfortable.

- Leave excess paraphernalia at home – Shopping bags and odd bundles will get in your way. You need bring only the items mentioned in the official notice you received; usually everything you need is provided. Do not bring reference books to the exam. They will only confuse those last minutes and be taken away from you when in the test room.
- Arrive somewhat ahead of time – If because of transportation schedules you must get there very early, bring a newspaper or magazine to take your mind off yourself while waiting.
- Locate the examination room – When you have found the proper room, you will be directed to the seat or part of the room where you will sit. Sometimes you are given a sheet of instructions to read while you are waiting. Do not fill out any forms until you are told to do so; just read them and be prepared.
- Relax and prepare to listen to the instructions
- If you have any physical problem that may keep you from doing your best, be sure to tell the test administrator. If you are sick or in poor health, you really cannot do your best on the exam. You can come back and take the test some other time.

VII. AT THE TEST

The day of the test is here and you have the test booklet in your hand. The temptation to get going is very strong. Caution! There is more to success than knowing the right answers. You must know how to identify your papers and understand variations in the type of short-answer question used in this particular examination. Follow these suggestions for maximum results from your efforts:

1) Cooperate with the monitor

The test administrator has a duty to create a situation in which you can be as much at ease as possible. He will give instructions, tell you when to begin, check to see that you are marking your answer sheet correctly, and so on. He is not there to guard you, although he will see that your competitors do not take unfair advantage. He wants to help you do your best.

2) Listen to all instructions

Don't jump the gun! Wait until you understand all directions. In most civil service tests you get more time than you need to answer the questions. So don't be in a hurry. Read each word of instructions until you clearly understand the meaning. Study the examples, listen to all announcements and follow directions. Ask questions if you do not understand what to do.

3) Identify your papers

Civil service exams are usually identified by number only. You will be assigned a number; you must not put your name on your test papers. Be sure to copy your number correctly. Since more than one exam may be given, copy your exact examination title.

4) Plan your time

Unless you are told that a test is a "speed" or "rate of work" test, speed itself is usually not important. Time enough to answer all the questions will be provided, but this does not mean that you have all day. An overall time limit has been set. Divide the total time (in minutes) by the number of questions to determine the approximate time you have for each question.

5) Do not linger over difficult questions

If you come across a difficult question, mark it with a paper clip (useful to have along) and come back to it when you have been through the booklet. One caution if you do this – be sure to skip a number on your answer sheet as well. Check often to be sure that you have not lost your place and that you are marking in the row numbered the same as the question you are answering.

6) Read the questions

Be sure you know what the question asks! Many capable people are unsuccessful because they failed to *read* the questions correctly.

7) Answer all questions

Unless you have been instructed that a penalty will be deducted for incorrect answers, it is better to guess than to omit a question.

8) Speed tests

It is often better NOT to guess on speed tests. It has been found that on timed tests people are tempted to spend the last few seconds before time is called in marking answers at random – without even reading them – in the hope of picking up a few extra points. To discourage this practice, the instructions may warn you that your score will be "corrected" for guessing. That is, a penalty will be applied. The incorrect answers will be deducted from the correct ones, or some other penalty formula will be used.

9) Review your answers

If you finish before time is called, go back to the questions you guessed or omitted to give them further thought. Review other answers if you have time.

10) Return your test materials

If you are ready to leave before others have finished or time is called, take ALL your materials to the monitor and leave quietly. Never take any test material with you. The monitor can discover whose papers are not complete, and taking a test booklet may be grounds for disqualification.

VIII. EXAMINATION TECHNIQUES

1) Read the general instructions carefully. These are usually printed on the first page of the exam booklet. As a rule, these instructions refer to the timing of the examination; the fact that you should not start work until the signal and must stop work at a signal, etc. If there are any *special* instructions, such as a choice of questions to be answered, make sure that you note this instruction carefully.

2) When you are ready to start work on the examination, that is as soon as the signal has been given, read the instructions to each question booklet, underline any key words or phrases, such as *least, best, outline, describe* and the like. In this way you will tend to answer as requested rather than discover on reviewing your paper that you *listed without describing*, that you selected the *worst* choice rather than the *best* choice, etc.

3) If the examination is of the objective or multiple-choice type – that is, each question will also give a series of possible answers: A, B, C or D, and you are called upon to select the best answer and write the letter next to that answer on your answer paper – it is advisable to start answering each question in turn. There may be anywhere from 50 to 100 such questions in the three or four hours allotted and you can see how much time would be taken if you read through all the questions before beginning to answer any. Furthermore, if you come across a question or group of questions which you know would be difficult to answer, it would undoubtedly affect your handling of all the other questions.

4) If the examination is of the essay type and contains but a few questions, it is a moot point as to whether you should read all the questions before starting to answer any one. Of course, if you are given a choice – say five out of seven and the like – then it is essential to read all the questions so you can eliminate the two that are most difficult. If, however, you are asked to answer all the questions, there may be danger in trying to answer the easiest one first because you may find that you will spend too much time on it. The best technique is to answer the first question, then proceed to the second, etc.

5) Time your answers. Before the exam begins, write down the time it started, then add the time allowed for the examination and write down the time it must be completed, then divide the time available somewhat as follows:
   - If 3-1/2 hours are allowed, that would be 210 minutes. If you have 80 objective-type questions, that would be an average of 2-1/2 minutes per question. Allow yourself no more than 2 minutes per question, or a total of 160 minutes, which will permit about 50 minutes to review.
   - If for the time allotment of 210 minutes there are 7 essay questions to answer, that would average about 30 minutes a question. Give yourself only 25 minutes per question so that you have about 35 minutes to review.

6) The most important instruction is to *read each question* and make sure you know what is wanted. The second most important instruction is to *time yourself properly* so that you answer every question. The third most important instruction is to *answer every question*. Guess if you have to but include something for each question. Remember that you will receive no credit for a blank and will probably receive some credit if you write something in answer to an essay question. If you guess a letter – say "B" for a multiple-choice question – you may have guessed right. If you leave a blank as an answer to a multiple-choice question, the examiners may respect your feelings but it will not add a point to your score. Some exams may penalize you for wrong answers, so in such cases *only*, you may not want to guess unless you have some basis for your answer.

7) Suggestions
   a. Objective-type questions
      1. Examine the question booklet for proper sequence of pages and questions
      2. Read all instructions carefully
      3. Skip any question which seems too difficult; return to it after all other questions have been answered
      4. Apportion your time properly; do not spend too much time on any single question or group of questions

5. Note and underline key words – *all, most, fewest, least, best, worst, same, opposite*, etc.
6. Pay particular attention to negatives
7. Note unusual option, e.g., unduly long, short, complex, different or similar in content to the body of the question
8. Observe the use of "hedging" words – *probably, may, most likely,* etc.
9. Make sure that your answer is put next to the same number as the question
10. Do not second-guess unless you have good reason to believe the second answer is definitely more correct
11. Cross out original answer if you decide another answer is more accurate; do not erase until you are ready to hand your paper in
12. Answer all questions; guess unless instructed otherwise
13. Leave time for review

b. Essay questions
   1. Read each question carefully
   2. Determine exactly what is wanted. Underline key words or phrases.
   3. Decide on outline or paragraph answer
   4. Include many different points and elements unless asked to develop any one or two points or elements
   5. Show impartiality by giving pros and cons unless directed to select one side only
   6. Make and write down any assumptions you find necessary to answer the questions
   7. Watch your English, grammar, punctuation and choice of words
   8. Time your answers; don't crowd material

8) Answering the essay question

Most essay questions can be answered by framing the specific response around several key words or ideas. Here are a few such key words or ideas:

M's: manpower, materials, methods, money, management
P's: purpose, program, policy, plan, procedure, practice, problems, pitfalls, personnel, public relations

   a. Six basic steps in handling problems:
      1. Preliminary plan and background development
      2. Collect information, data and facts
      3. Analyze and interpret information, data and facts
      4. Analyze and develop solutions as well as make recommendations
      5. Prepare report and sell recommendations
      6. Install recommendations and follow up effectiveness

   b. Pitfalls to avoid
      1. *Taking things for granted* – A statement of the situation does not necessarily imply that each of the elements is necessarily true; for example, a complaint may be invalid and biased so that all that can be taken for granted is that a complaint has been registered

2. *Considering only one side of a situation* – Wherever possible, indicate several alternatives and then point out the reasons you selected the best one
3. *Failing to indicate follow up* – Whenever your answer indicates action on your part, make certain that you will take proper follow-up action to see how successful your recommendations, procedures or actions turn out to be
4. *Taking too long in answering any single question* – Remember to time your answers properly

IX. AFTER THE TEST

Scoring procedures differ in detail among civil service jurisdictions although the general principles are the same. Whether the papers are hand-scored or graded by machine we have described, they are nearly always graded by number. That is, the person who marks the paper knows only the number – never the name – of the applicant. Not until all the papers have been graded will they be matched with names. If other tests, such as training and experience or oral interview ratings have been given, scores will be combined. Different parts of the examination usually have different weights. For example, the written test might count 60 percent of the final grade, and a rating of training and experience 40 percent. In many jurisdictions, veterans will have a certain number of points added to their grades.

After the final grade has been determined, the names are placed in grade order and an eligible list is established. There are various methods for resolving ties between those who get the same final grade – probably the most common is to place first the name of the person whose application was received first. Job offers are made from the eligible list in the order the names appear on it. You will be notified of your grade and your rank as soon as all these computations have been made. This will be done as rapidly as possible.

People who are found to meet the requirements in the announcement are called "eligibles." Their names are put on a list of eligible candidates. An eligible's chances of getting a job depend on how high he stands on this list and how fast agencies are filling jobs from the list.

When a job is to be filled from a list of eligibles, the agency asks for the names of people on the list of eligibles for that job. When the civil service commission receives this request, it sends to the agency the names of the three people highest on this list. Or, if the job to be filled has specialized requirements, the office sends the agency the names of the top three persons who meet these requirements from the general list.

The appointing officer makes a choice from among the three people whose names were sent to him. If the selected person accepts the appointment, the names of the others are put back on the list to be considered for future openings.

That is the rule in hiring from all kinds of eligible lists, whether they are for typist, carpenter, chemist, or something else. For every vacancy, the appointing officer has his choice of any one of the top three eligibles on the list. This explains why the person whose name is on top of the list sometimes does not get an appointment when some of the persons lower on the list do. If the appointing officer chooses the second or third eligible, the No. 1 eligible does not get a job at once, but stays on the list until he is appointed or the list is terminated.

X. HOW TO PASS THE INTERVIEW TEST

The examination for which you applied requires an oral interview test. You have already taken the written test and you are now being called for the interview test – the final part of the formal examination.

You may think that it is not possible to prepare for an interview test and that there are no procedures to follow during an interview. Our purpose is to point out some things you can do in advance that will help you and some good rules to follow and pitfalls to avoid while you are being interviewed.

What is an interview supposed to test?

The written examination is designed to test the technical knowledge and competence of the candidate; the oral is designed to evaluate intangible qualities, not readily measured otherwise, and to establish a list showing the relative fitness of each candidate – as measured against his competitors – for the position sought. Scoring is not on the basis of "right" and "wrong," but on a sliding scale of values ranging from "not passable" to "outstanding." As a matter of fact, it is possible to achieve a relatively low score without a single "incorrect" answer because of evident weakness in the qualities being measured.

Occasionally, an examination may consist entirely of an oral test – either an individual or a group oral. In such cases, information is sought concerning the technical knowledges and abilities of the candidate, since there has been no written examination for this purpose. More commonly, however, an oral test is used to supplement a written examination.

Who conducts interviews?

The composition of oral boards varies among different jurisdictions. In nearly all, a representative of the personnel department serves as chairman. One of the members of the board may be a representative of the department in which the candidate would work. In some cases, "outside experts" are used, and, frequently, a businessman or some other representative of the general public is asked to serve. Labor and management or other special groups may be represented. The aim is to secure the services of experts in the appropriate field.

However the board is composed, it is a good idea (and not at all improper or unethical) to ascertain in advance of the interview who the members are and what groups they represent. When you are introduced to them, you will have some idea of their backgrounds and interests, and at least you will not stutter and stammer over their names.

What should be done before the interview?

While knowledge about the board members is useful and takes some of the surprise element out of the interview, there is other preparation which is more substantive. It *is* possible to prepare for an oral interview – in several ways:

1) Keep a copy of your application and review it carefully before the interview

This may be the only document before the oral board, and the starting point of the interview. Know what education and experience you have listed there, and the sequence and dates of all of it. Sometimes the board will ask you to review the highlights of your experience for them; you should not have to hem and haw doing it.

2) Study the class specification and the examination announcement

Usually, the oral board has one or both of these to guide them. The qualities, characteristics or knowledges required by the position sought are stated in these documents. They offer valuable clues as to the nature of the oral interview. For example, if the job involves supervisory responsibilities, the announcement will usually indicate that knowledge of modern supervisory methods and the qualifications of the candidate as a supervisor will be tested. If so, you can expect such questions, frequently in the form of a hypothetical situation which you are expected to solve. NEVER go into an oral without knowledge of the duties and responsibilities of the job you seek.

3) Think through each qualification required

Try to visualize the kind of questions you would ask if you were a board member. How well could you answer them? Try especially to appraise your own knowledge and background in each area, *measured against the job sought*, and identify any areas in which you are weak. Be critical and realistic – do not flatter yourself.

4) Do some general reading in areas in which you feel you may be weak

For example, if the job involves supervision and your past experience has NOT, some general reading in supervisory methods and practices, particularly in the field of human relations, might be useful. Do NOT study agency procedures or detailed manuals. The oral board will be testing your understanding and capacity, not your memory.

5) Get a good night's sleep and watch your general health and mental attitude

You will want a clear head at the interview. Take care of a cold or any other minor ailment, and of course, no hangovers.

What should be done on the day of the interview?

Now comes the day of the interview itself. Give yourself plenty of time to get there. Plan to arrive somewhat ahead of the scheduled time, particularly if your appointment is in the fore part of the day. If a previous candidate fails to appear, the board might be ready for you a bit early. By early afternoon an oral board is almost invariably behind schedule if there are many candidates, and you may have to wait. Take along a book or magazine to read, or your application to review, but leave any extraneous material in the waiting room when you go in for your interview. In any event, relax and compose yourself.

The matter of dress is important. The board is forming impressions about you – from your experience, your manners, your attitude, and your appearance. Give your personal appearance careful attention. Dress your best, but not your flashiest. Choose conservative, appropriate clothing, and be sure it is immaculate. This is a business interview, and your appearance should indicate that you regard it as such. Besides, being well groomed and properly dressed will help boost your confidence.

Sooner or later, someone will call your name and escort you into the interview room. *This is it.* From here on you are on your own. It is too late for any more preparation. But remember, you asked for this opportunity to prove your fitness, and you are here because your request was granted.

What happens when you go in?

The usual sequence of events will be as follows: The clerk (who is often the board stenographer) will introduce you to the chairman of the oral board, who will introduce you to the other members of the board. Acknowledge the introductions before you sit down. Do not be surprised if you find a microphone facing you or a stenotypist sitting by. Oral interviews are usually recorded in the event of an appeal or other review.

Usually the chairman of the board will open the interview by reviewing the highlights of your education and work experience from your application – primarily for the benefit of the other members of the board, as well as to get the material into the record. Do not interrupt or comment unless there is an error or significant misinterpretation; if that is the case, do not hesitate. But do not quibble about insignificant matters. Also, he will usually ask you some question about your education, experience or your present job – partly to get you to start talking and to establish the interviewing "rapport." He may start the actual questioning, or turn it over to one of the other members. Frequently, each member undertakes the questioning on a particular area, one in which he is perhaps most competent, so you can expect each member to participate in the examination. Because time is limited, you may also expect some rather abrupt switches in the direction the questioning takes, so do not be upset by it. Normally, a board member will not pursue a single line of questioning unless he discovers a particular strength or weakness.

After each member has participated, the chairman will usually ask whether any member has any further questions, then will ask you if you have anything you wish to add. Unless you are expecting this question, it may floor you. Worse, it may start you off on an extended, extemporaneous speech. The board is not usually seeking more information. The question is principally to offer you a last opportunity to present further qualifications or to indicate that you have nothing to add. So, if you feel that a significant qualification or characteristic has been overlooked, it is proper to point it out in a sentence or so. Do not compliment the board on the thoroughness of their examination – they have been sketchy, and you know it. If you wish, merely say, "No thank you, I have nothing further to add." This is a point where you can "talk yourself out" of a good impression or fail to present an important bit of information. Remember, *you close the interview yourself*.

The chairman will then say, "That is all, Mr. _____, thank you." Do not be startled; the interview is over, and quicker than you think. Thank him, gather your belongings and take your leave. Save your sigh of relief for the other side of the door.

How to put your best foot forward

Throughout this entire process, you may feel that the board individually and collectively is trying to pierce your defenses, seek out your hidden weaknesses and embarrass and confuse you. Actually, this is not true. They are obliged to make an appraisal of your qualifications for the job you are seeking, and they want to see you in your best light. Remember, they must interview all candidates and a non-cooperative candidate may become a failure in spite of their best efforts to bring out his qualifications. Here are 15 suggestions that will help you:

1) Be natural – Keep your attitude confident, not cocky

If you are not confident that you can do the job, do not expect the board to be. Do not apologize for your weaknesses, try to bring out your strong points. The board is interested in a positive, not negative, presentation. Cockiness will antagonize any board member and make him wonder if you are covering up a weakness by a false show of strength.

2) Get comfortable, but don't lounge or sprawl

Sit erectly but not stiffly. A careless posture may lead the board to conclude that you are careless in other things, or at least that you are not impressed by the importance of the occasion. Either conclusion is natural, even if incorrect. Do not fuss with your clothing, a pencil or an ashtray. Your hands may occasionally be useful to emphasize a point; do not let them become a point of distraction.

3) Do not wisecrack or make small talk

This is a serious situation, and your attitude should show that you consider it as such. Further, the time of the board is limited – they do not want to waste it, and neither should you.

4) Do not exaggerate your experience or abilities

In the first place, from information in the application or other interviews and sources, the board may know more about you than you think. Secondly, you probably will not get away with it. An experienced board is rather adept at spotting such a situation, so do not take the chance.

5) If you know a board member, do not make a point of it, yet do not hide it

Certainly you are not fooling him, and probably not the other members of the board. Do not try to take advantage of your acquaintanceship – it will probably do you little good.

6) Do not dominate the interview

Let the board do that. They will give you the clues – do not assume that you have to do all the talking. Realize that the board has a number of questions to ask you, and do not try to take up all the interview time by showing off your extensive knowledge of the answer to the first one.

7) Be attentive

You only have 20 minutes or so, and you should keep your attention at its sharpest throughout. When a member is addressing a problem or question to you, give him your undivided attention. Address your reply principally to him, but do not exclude the other board members.

8) Do not interrupt

A board member may be stating a problem for you to analyze. He will ask you a question when the time comes. Let him state the problem, and wait for the question.

9) Make sure you understand the question

Do not try to answer until you are sure what the question is. If it is not clear, restate it in your own words or ask the board member to clarify it for you. However, do not haggle about minor elements.

10) Reply promptly but not hastily

A common entry on oral board rating sheets is "candidate responded readily," or "candidate hesitated in replies." Respond as promptly and quickly as you can, but do not jump to a hasty, ill-considered answer.

11) Do not be peremptory in your answers

A brief answer is proper – but do not fire your answer back. That is a losing game from your point of view. The board member can probably ask questions much faster than you can answer them.

12) Do not try to create the answer you think the board member wants

He is interested in what kind of mind you have and how it works – not in playing games. Furthermore, he can usually spot this practice and will actually grade you down on it.

13) Do not switch sides in your reply merely to agree with a board member

Frequently, a member will take a contrary position merely to draw you out and to see if you are willing and able to defend your point of view. Do not start a debate, yet do not surrender a good position. If a position is worth taking, it is worth defending.

14) Do not be afraid to admit an error in judgment if you are shown to be wrong

The board knows that you are forced to reply without any opportunity for careful consideration. Your answer may be demonstrably wrong. If so, admit it and get on with the interview.

15) Do not dwell at length on your present job

The opening question may relate to your present assignment. Answer the question but do not go into an extended discussion. You are being examined for a *new* job, not your present one. As a matter of fact, try to phrase ALL your answers in terms of the job for which you are being examined.

Basis of Rating

Probably you will forget most of these "do's" and "don'ts" when you walk into the oral interview room. Even remembering them all will not ensure you a passing grade. Perhaps you did not have the qualifications in the first place. But remembering them will help you to put your best foot forward, without treading on the toes of the board members.

Rumor and popular opinion to the contrary notwithstanding, an oral board wants you to make the best appearance possible. They know you are under pressure – but they also want to see how you respond to it as a guide to what your reaction would be under the pressures of the job you seek. They will be influenced by the degree of poise you display, the personal traits you show and the manner in which you respond.

ABOUT THIS BOOK

This book contains tests divided into Examination Sections. Go through each test, answering every question in the margin. We have also attached a sample answer sheet at the back of the book that can be removed and used. At the end of each test look at the answer key and check your answers. On the ones you got wrong, look at the right answer choice and learn. Do not fill in the answers first. Do not memorize the questions and answers, but understand the answer and principles involved. On your test, the questions will likely be different from the samples. Questions are changed and new ones added. If you understand these past questions you should have success with any changes that arise. Tests may consist of several types of questions. We have additional books on each subject should more study be advisable or necessary for you. Finally, the more you study, the better prepared you will be. This book is intended to be the last thing you study before you walk into the examination room. Prior study of relevant texts is also recommended. NLC publishes some of these in our Fundamental Series. Knowledge and good sense are important factors in passing your exam. Good luck also helps. So now study this Passbook, absorb the material contained within and take that knowledge into the examination. Then do your best to pass that exam.

EXAMINATION SECTION

EXAMINATION SECTION
TEST 1

DIRECTIONS: Each question or incomplete statement is followed by several suggested answers or completions. Select the one that BEST answers the question or completes the statement. *PRINT THE LETTER OF THE CORRECT ANSWER IN THE SPACE AT THE RIGHT.*

1. If in doubt as to the meaning of any rule, regulation, or instruction, the BEST procedure for a train operator to follow is to
   A. ask another train operator for an explanation
   B. obtain an explanation from the dispatcher
   C. use their best judgment when a situation arises
   D. discuss the matter with the conductor

   1._____

2. Before leaving his/her train for any reason, a conduct must FIRST
   A. pass one long buzzer to the train operator
   B. pass one long, one short, one long, and one short buzzer to the train operator
   C. open an emergency brake valve
   D. tell the train operator on the P.A. or intercom that he/she is leaving the train

   2._____

3. A conductor must not close the doors of a train in the station until they have been fully opened for at least
   A. five seconds
   B. ten seconds
   C. five seconds in the front and ten seconds in the rear
   D. ten seconds in the front and five seconds in the rear

   3._____

4. If a train operator, without authorization, fails to make a scheduled station stop, the conductor must FIRST
   A. pass one long buzzer to the train operator
   B. operate an emergency brake valve at the next station that the train stops at and find out why the train operator skipped a station
   C. immediately operate an emergency brake valve
   D. notify the Control Center and investigate the cause

   4._____

5. How many minutes before the scheduled leaving time must the train operator be on the train with all train identification equipment properly displayed and in place?
   A. One   B. Two   C. Four   D. Five

   5._____

6. When making a station stop, a train operator must stop the first car of the train
   A. wherever the train operator thinks that all of the cars are in the station
   B. always with the head car opposite the end of the station platform
   C. at least 15 feet from the signal located at the end of the platform
   D. opposite the proper station car stop sign for the length of the train

6.____

7. If the train whistle/horn becomes inoperative enroute, and the problem cannot be corrected, the train operator must
   A. proceed cautiously and report the condition at the first opportunity
   B. have the conductor blow the whistle
   C. operate from the second car
   D. call the Control Center, then proceed at restricted speed with extreme caution to the next station and discharge customers

7.____

8. A train operator observing that the tower operator has set up the wrong route should signal with _____ whistle blast(s).
   A. one long   B. two short   C. three short   D. four short

8.____

9. When a train operator sounds three short blasts on the train whistle, he/she is
   A. signaling for a transit police officer
   B. warning customers standing too close to the platform edge
   C. calling for the road car inspector
   D. acknowledging a lantern signal

9.____

10. A train operator, operating in a yard, hearing one long blast on the tower whistle knows that the tower operator is signaling for
    A. all trains within the interlocking limits to come to an immediate stop
    B. the yard dispatcher to come to the tower
    C. a train on the yard lead to enter the yard
    D. a signal maintainer to call the field office

10.____

11. When a train bypasses a station platform, the train operator must
    A. not operate his train faster than 15 mph leaving the station
    B. blow horn/whistle upon entering and leaving the station
    C. enter the station at the normal speed for the area
    D. all of the above

11.____

12. An *absolute block* is a
    A. section of track that is blocked off from any train movement
    B. metal or concrete block that is placed at the end of a lay-up track
    C. section of track that can be occupied by no more than two trains at a time
    D. section of track that can be occupied by no more than two trains at a time

12.____

13. An *interlocking* is
    A. the two ends of a track that are connected by a joint bar
    B. a section or sections of track where the signals and switches are controlled by a tower
    C. the part of the coupler that locks with the coupler of another car
    D. a metal plate that connects an elevated section of track to a trestle

14. A *timetable* is
    A. the authority for the movement of regular trains in passenger service
    B. the amount of time that is allowed to make up a train in a yard
    C. the time it takes for a work train to go from one yard to another
    D. a list of allowable times required to make different moves in a yard

15. A train operator must accept a route from the express to local track if the
    A. running time is the same
    B. conductor orders the train operator to make local stops
    C. train operator determines that local stops must be made because the local train broke down
    D. local route does not divert him/her from their scheduled line

16. Train operators report to
    A. assistant train dispatchers, dispatchers, and car equipment supervisors
    B. superintendents (RTO), signal maintainers, train service supervisors
    C. yard dispatchers, road car inspectors, assistant train dispatchers
    D. train dispatchers, superintendents (RTO), yard dispatchers

17. Train operators must observe that there is sufficient air by examining the duplex air gauge
    A. in every instance before starting a train
    B. before rounding curves
    C. before approaching descending grades
    D. all of the above

18. If, for any reason, some side doors of the train fail to open, the conductor must allow _____ for customers to detrain and entrain.
    A. thirty seconds
    B. ample opportunity
    C. twenty seconds
    D. fifteen seconds in the rear section and twenty seconds in the front section

19. If a train operator must leave his/her train while enroute, it is only necessary to secure the train
    A. if left on a downgrade
    B. if left on an upgrade
    C. the train must always be secured
    D. if left in between stations with customers aboard

20. A train may run ahead of schedule if
    A. the conductor orders the train operator to keep moving
    B. in the opinion of the train operator, this can be done safely
    C. ordered to do so by the proper authority
    D. all signals are green and there are no speed signs or other speed restrictions

21. A proceed hand signal may never be given with a _____ lantern.
    A. white   B. green   C. yellow   D. red

22. A signal which is never clear but always displays a red aspect is a _____ signal.
    A. home   B. grade time C. automatic   D. marker

Questions 23-40.

DIRECTIONS: Questions 23 through 40 are to be answered on the basis of the accompanying illustrations of aspects of signals, signs, and markers used on the transit system. In the illustrations, "G" denotes a green aspect illuminated, "Y" denotes yellow aspect illuminated, "R" denotes red aspect illuminated, and "S" denotes an illuminated S aspect.

23. This signal indicates:
    A. stop and call
    B. stop and then proceed, prepared to stop within vision
    C. approach with caution at allowable speed
    D. stop, and after authorization, proceed with restricted speed and extreme caution according to Rule #40(n)

24. This signal indicates:
    A. stop and stay
    B. stop and then proceed, prepared to stop within vision
    C. approach with caution at allowable speed and the next signal will clear
    D. approach with caution

25. The indication of this signal is:
    A. proceed with caution
    B. stop and then proceed, prepared to stop within vision
    C. proceed with caution at allowable speed
    D. proceed

26. This signal means:
    A. stop and then proceed, prepared to stop within vision
    B. proceed with caution, prepared to stop at next signal
    C. proceed with caution at allowable speed
    D. proceed, expecting to find track occupied

26.____

27. The indication of this illuminated sign is:
    A. graded thru-span 10 yards beyond the sign
    B. beginning of grade timing section at the indicated speed
    C. take turnout at indicated speed
    D. station platform telephone

27.____

28. This sign means that:
    A. there are no speed restrictions beyond this point
    B. signals beyond this point do not apply to trains
    C. train operator may operate without regard to rules beyond this point
    D. there are no electrically operated signals beyond this point

28.____

29. The non-illuminated sign shown is the:
    A. station car stop sign for 6-car trains
    B. turning point marker for 6-car trains
    C. beginning of coasting marker for 6-car train
    D. marker for the point at which a 6-car train may resume normal speed

29.____

30. This sign means:
    A. station car stop sign for 4-car trains
    B. reverse move for 4-car trains
    C. beginning of coasting marker for 4-car trains
    D. marker for the point at which a 4-car train may resume normal speed

30.____

31. This signal aspect means:
    A. proceed normally on either route
    B. proceed, not exceeding 25 mph on main route
    C. proceed normally on diverging route
    D. proceed at allowable speed on main route

31.____

32. This signal indicates:
    A. proceed on diverging route expecting next signal to be red
    B. proceed on main route expecting next signal to be red
    C. proceed on diverging route expecting next signal to be clear
    D. proceed on main route expecting next signal to be clear

32.____

33. This signal aspect means:
    A. stop and operate the route request button, then proceed
    B. stop, operate stop release, then proceed with caution
    C. stop and stay
    D. stop and key by signal

33.____

34. This signal aspect means:
    A. proceed on diverging route expecting next signal to be red
    B. proceed on main route expecting next signal to be red
    C. proceed on diverging route expecting next signal to be clear
    D. proceed on main route expecting next signal to be clear

34.____

35. This aspect means
    A. proceed on main route
    B. proceed with caution on diverging route, be prepared to stop at next signal
    C. proceed on diverging route
    D. proceed, prepared to stop at next signal on main route

35.____

36. This signal aspect means:
    A. stop and signal for route
    B. stop, operate automatic stop, manual release, observe automatic stop arm go down fully, then proceed with restricted speed and extreme caution
    C. stop and wait for a less restrictive aspect
    D. stop and telephone for orders

36.____

37. This aspect means:
    A. operate the stop release and then proceed with caution
    B. operate the hand throw switch and then proceed with caution
    C. enter inspection shed with caution
    D. yard indication signal used in place of call-on

37.____

38. This sign indicates:
    A. station car stop sign for 6-car trains
    B. turning point marker for 6-car trains
    C. beginning of coasting marker for 6-car trains
    D. a point at which a 6-car train may resume allowable speed

38.____

39. A fouling point sign is used to
    A. inform a train operator that a switch is "Out of Service"
    B. define the clearance point at hand-operated switches
    C. indicate a move for a facing point switch only
    D. indicate a move for a trailing point switch only

39.____

40. This signal aspect means:
    A. proceed with caution prepared to stop within vision, expecting to find track occupied
    B. proceed with caution, next signal is clear
    C. proceed with caution on diverging route
    D. proceed into yard lead or siding

40.____

KEY (CORRECT ANSWERS)

1.	B	11.	D	21.	D	31.	D
2.	C	12.	C	22.	D	32.	A
3.	B	13.	B	23.	A	33.	C
4.	C	14.	A	24.	C	34.	C
5.	B	15.	D	25.	D	35.	D
6.	D	16.	D	26.	B	36.	B
7.	D	17.	D	27.	B	37.	D
8.	D	18.	B	28.	D	38.	D
9.	C	19.	C	29.	A	39.	B
10.	A	20.	C	30.	B	40.	A

TEST 2

DIRECTIONS: Each question or incomplete statement is followed by several suggested answers or completions. Select the one that BEST answers the question or completes the statement. *PRINT THE LETTER OF THE CORRECT ANSWER IN THE SPACE AT THE RIGHT.*

1. The train operator whistle signal to call for assistance is   1.____
   A. long-short-long-short   B. short-long-short-long
   C. short-short-short   D. long-long-long

2. Block signals which are normally at danger and which enforce train operation at a predetermined reduced speed are classified as _____ signals.   2.____
   A. G.T.   B. S.T.   C. approach   D. dwarf

Questions 3-8.

DIRECTIONS: Questions 3 through 8 are to be answered on the basis of the following paragraph entitled *Procedure For Flagging Disabled Train*. Consult the paragraph when answering these questions.

PROCEDURE FOR FLAGGING DISABLED TRAIN

A train operator shall not operate a passenger train from other than the leading car without a duly authorized Rapid Transit Operations supervisor in charge of the operations. Desk Superintendent must be immediately notified. Rapid Transit Operations supervisor shall first establish by actual test a positive means of communication between a qualified Rapid Transit Operations employee on the head end of the first car and the train operator. Communication by sound powered telephone or radio shall be used. If sound powered telephone or radio becomes inoperative, necessary additional qualified employees can be utilized to establish positive communication. Light, hand or buzzer signals must not be used as means of communication for this operation. Speed of train under this condition shall not exceed ten miles per hour, or shall the controller be advanced beyond series position. The train operator must not start his/her train until he/she is sure it is safe to move. Train operator must wait for the proper signal from the employee on the front of the train. The train operator running the train must continue to receive and answer voice signals from the employee at the front end while the train is moving. If the signals stop at any time, the flagger or train operator must immediately stop the train and find out why.

3. The qualified employee stationed at the forward end must not be a   3.____
   A. train operator   B. conductor
   C. train service supervisor   D. road car inspector

4. While the train is in motion, the employee stationed at the forward end must give a flagging signal   4.____
   A. continuously
   B. every time the train is about to pass a fixed signal
   C. only when the train speed is changed
   D. only when they want to check their understanding with the train operator

9

2 (#2)

5. The train operator operating from other than the leading car must not advance   5.____
   the controller beyond
   A. switching   B. series   C. multiple   D. parallel

6. Considering the actual conditions on customer train in the subway, the MOST   6.____
   practical method of communication between the train operator and the
   employee at the forward end, would be using the
   A. radio   B. buzzer signals
   C. whistle signals   D. light signals

7. The BEST reason for discharging customers at the next station under these   7.____
   conditions is that
   A. carrying customers would cause additional delays
   B. it is not possible to operate safely
   C. the train operator cannot see the station stop markers
   D. the four lights at the front of the train will be red

8. When operating from other than the front end of a train, if a train operator   8.____
   does not receive a proceed signal at short intervals, while the train is in
   motion, the BEST action to follow would be to
   A. assume the most likely meaning
   B. proceed cautiously
   C. stop immediately
   D. disregard communications entirely

9. A single track operation means: 9.____
   A. a monorail operation
   B. trains will run in both directions on one track
   C. no married pair of cars are to operate on this track
   D. there are no switches involved in this operation

10. A train operator operating in the subway approaching a home signal displaying   10.____
    stop observes a man standing near the signal waving a white lantern up and
    down. The train operator stops the train at the signal, recognizes that the
    man waving the lantern is the section signal maintainer and proceeds with
    restricted speed and extreme caution.
    In this situation, the train operator should have
    A. called the Control Center Desk Superintendent
    B. proceeded without stopping
    C. blow the horn twice, then proceed at normal speed
    D. proceed exactly as outlined

11. The BEST way for train operators to acquaint themselves with new regulations   11.____
    as soon as possible is to
    A. study the Book of Rules
    B. depend on specific notice by the train service supervisor
    C. be alert to the needs of the service
    D. read all bulletins as issued

12. If a train operator receives a poorly executed hand or lantern signal that he/she is not positive of the meaning, the BEST action for him/her to follow would be to
    A. assume the most likely meaning
    B. proceed cautiously
    C. stop immediately
    D. disregard the signal entirely

13. When a train operator reads a General Order stating that a certain track will be operated as an *absolute block* between two specified point, he/she should know that on this particular track
    A. only one train at a time may be between the specified points
    B. trains will proceed on hand signals only
    C. only one direction of traffic will be allowed
    D. alternate trains will run in opposite directions

14. On bringing his/her train to a stop at an unattended red lantern adjacent to his/her track, a train operator must
    A. proceed with caution after seeing that the track ahead is clear
    B. pick up the lantern and proceed, reporting the incident to the first dispatcher he/she sees
    C. call the Control Center Desk Superintendent for orders
    D. blow a series of short blasts and then proceed with caution

15. A train operator finds a male customer asleep on a train he/she had just laid up in the yard. The BEST action for the train operator to take is to
    A. escort the customer to the nearest yard gate and let him out
    B. take the customer to crew quarters so that he can leave with the next man clearing
    C. move the customer to the end car, cut it off, and run it back to the terminal
    D. stay with the customer and signal for a yard employee to notify the Yard Dispatcher

16. At a blue light location in the subway, you would not ordinarily expect to find an emergency
    A. alarm box
    B. telephone
    C. fire extinguisher
    D. exit

17. When an emergency alarm box in the subway is pulled, power will be removed from the third rail and, in addition,
    A. an alarm will be sounded in the nearest firehouse
    B. the local telephone will be connected directly to the Control Center Desk superintendent's office
    C. an alarm will be sounded in the Control Center Desk Superintendent's office
    D. the brakes on all trains in the area will apply in emergency

18. While a train is braking to a regular stop at a passenger station, third rail power fails. The train operator would surely become aware of this failure when
    A. his/her brakes applied in emergency automatically
    B. he/she tried to start after the station stop
    C. the train stopped short of the car stop marker
    D. the train stopped beyond the car stop marker

19. After being signaled to slow down by lanterns because men are working on the tracks, a train operator should expect to see a signal beyond the work area indicating that he/she can resume speed.
    This signal should be placed beyond the work area a distance of
    A. 550 feet on Subdivision "A", 750 feet on Subdivision "B"
    B. 400 feet on Subdivision "A", 500 feet on Subdivision "B"
    C. 300 feet
    D. at least maximum length of train permitted on the subdivision

20. The color of the signal which indicates to the train operator that he/she must slow down is
    A. red   B. white   C. blue   D. yellow

21. During an emergency evacuation to the trackway, benchwall, or to a train on an adjacent track, third rail power must be
    A. left on so the customers can see where they are going
    B. left on *only* if the Fire Department is on the scene
    C. turned off
    D. turned off *only* if the evacuation is to the trackway

22. The train operator and conductor must evacuate the customers immediately if
    A. the Fire Department takes longer than five minutes to arrive at the scene
    B. there is imminent danger to the safety of the customers
    C. the Transit Police cannot arrive at the scene within five minutes
    D. there are no Rapid Transit Operations supervisors that can arrive at the scene within five minutes

23. Handbrakes are to be applied on a train stopped on a grade. It would be BEST to apply the handbrakes on the cars
    A. on the upgrade on end
    B. with two handbrakes on each end of the train
    C. on the downgrade end
    D. on alternate cars on the entire train

24. After applying the required number of handbrakes on a train which has been parked on steep grade, the PROPER test of whether the handbrakes will hold the train is to
    A. apply the brakes in emergency
    B. examine each handbrake chain to see that it is tight
    C. release air brakes; apply one point of power
    D. open the compressor switches

25. Handbrakes should be set up on a train when the 25.____
    A. third rail power will be off 30 minutes or more
    B. train has stopped on a grade at a home signal indicating *Stop and Stay*
    C. train operator is changing ends at a terminal
    D. electric brake is cut out

26. When cars are being moved to be coupled together, the train operator must 26.____
    stop at least two car lengths, then fifty feet, then ten feet, then two feet from
    the standing cars, then moved
    A. 1/2 miles per hour   B. 2 miles per hour
    C. slowly with caution   D. 10 miles per hour

27. When making the prescribed brake test upon leaving a terminal, a train 27.____
    operator notices that the train does not roll freely when the controller is
    moved to the first point and then shut off.
    The BEST course of action in this case is to
    A. stop, apply sufficient handbrakes, and call the car inspector
    B. notch up the controller and try again at a higher speed
    C. discharge customers and take the train to the yard
    D. stop, and have the conductor help check to see that all handbrakes are
       properly released

28. When cars are retarded by means of dynamic braking, the dynamic braking 28.____
    will start to *fade* at approximately _____ MPH.
    A. 5   B. 10   C. 15   D. 20

29. The black hand of the duplex air gauge on any type of subway car indicates 29.____
    the air pressure in the
    A. brake pipe   B. straight air pipe
    C. main air line   D. brake cylinder

30. Before a train operator couples cars together, he must be sure that the 30.____
    couplers to be joined are aligned and that their electric portions are fully
    _____ and their shutters are _____.
    A. retrieved; closed   B. retrieved; open
    C. extended; closed   D. extended; open

31. The *electric portion* is part of the 31.____
    A. electro-pneumatic brake   B. master controller
    C. coupler   D. door engine

32. When the ME-43 brake valve handle is in its extreme right-hand position, 32.____
    the brake valve is in
    A. release   B. service   C. handle off   D. emergency

33. A train operator stops his/her local train at a home signal indicated *stop*. If his/her train is on an upgrade, the train operator should
    A. apply light handbrake
    B. keep the full service brake applied
    C. graduate off the air brake until the train just begins to roll
    D. apply the brake in emergency

34. The brakes on SMEE cars will not apply in emergency if the master controller handle is released when the reverser handle is forward and the brake vale is in
    A. full release
    B. full service
    C. running release
    D. handle off

35. On the SMEE-type subway car, the PROPER position of the brake handle when operating normally over the road is
    A. running release
    B. electric holding
    C. pneumatic service
    D. handle off

36. According to the latest instructions, before moving SMEE cars, the MINIMUM brake pipe pressure and the straight air pipe pressure should be, respectively,
    A. 90 and 72-80 pounds
    B. 80 and 60 pounds
    C. 70 and 90 pounds
    D. 60 and 90 pounds

37. The cutting-key is MOST closely associated in operation with a
    A. brake valve
    B. master controller
    C. contact shoe
    D. coupler

38. A train being brought to a stop from a speed of 30 MPH would be LEAST likely to skid if the track is
    A. slightly rusted and dry
    B. slightly rusted and wet
    C. well polished and wet
    D. well polished and dry

39. Route request buttons are installed on certain signals where there is a choice of route. If the signal indicated stop, the train operator can request the correct route by stopping at the signal and
    A. sounding three short whistle blasts
    B. telephoning the Signal Department
    C. pressing the button corresponding to the desired route
    D. pressing the button a number of times to correspond with the number of the route requested

40. One component which is NOT present on both cars of a *married pair* is a
    A. train operator's cab
    B. storage battery
    C. handbrake
    D. door control station

KEY (CORRECT ANSWERS)

1.	A	11.	D	21.	C	31.	C
2.	A	12.	C	22.	B	32.	C
3.	D	13.	A	23.	C	33.	B
4.	A	14.	C	24.	C	34.	B
5.	B	15.	D	25.	A	35.	A
6.	A	16.	D	26.	C	36.	A
7.	A	17.	C	27.	D	37.	D
8.	C	18.	B	28.	B	38.	D
9.	B	19.	D	29.	A	39.	C
10.	A	20.	D	30.	A	40.	B

TEST 3

DIRECTIONS: Each question or incomplete statement is followed by several suggested answers or completions. Select the one that BEST answers the question or completes the statement. *PRINT THE LETTER OF THE CORRECT ANSWER IN THE SPACE AT THE RIGHT.*

1. The part of the brake system which is designed to cause the brakes on all cars in a train to apply equally and at the same time is the
    A. equalizing valve
    B. dynamic brake
    C. protection reservoir
    D. electric brake circuit

    1.____

2. How many contact shoes are there on a SMEE car?
    A. One   B. Two   C. Three   D. Four

    2.____

3. R44 and up cars have _____ horsepower traction motors.
    A. two 400   B. two 600   C. four 75   D. four 115

    3.____

4. The train operator controls the train's propulsion system by
    A. automatic train control pushbuttons
    B. the brake valve handle
    C. the reverser key
    D. the master controller handle

    4.____

5. The master controller *switching* position is to be used
    A. only when arriving at the terminal
    B. only when going up hills
    C. only when going down hills
    D. when coupling and uncoupling cars

    5.____

6. The *deadman feature* applies emergency brakes
    A. in inclement weather
    B. from wayside trips when tripped
    C. if hand pressure is removed from the master controller handle while the brake valve handle is in full release or running release position
    D. when the train is in layover condition

    6.____

7. The brake valve handle is
    A. removable in all positions
    B. not removable
    C. removable only in the *handle off* position
    D. removable only in the *full service* position

    7.____

8. The handbrake indicator light on the train operator's auxiliary control panel illuminates
    A. when all handbrakes on the train are not applied
    B. when any handbrake on the train is applied
    C. when service brakes on the train are applied
    D. all of the above

    8.____

9. The duplex air gauge measures
   A. brake cylinder pressure
   B. only straight air pipe pressure (S.A.P.)
   C. only brake pipe pressure (B.P.)
   D. straight air pipe (S.A.P.) and brake pipe pressure (B.P.)

10. The emergency brake valve (EBV) causes an emergency brake application when actuated from
    A. the master controller
    B. the "A" side MDC of the operating cab
    C. either of the two pull cables located in the customer area and the cab area
    D. Central Control

11. An emergency brake application may be applied to
    A. placing the brake valve handle in the emergency position
    B. energizing the *deadman feature* by releasing hand pressure on the master controller handle while the handle is in an operating position and the brake valve handle is in either the full release or running release position
    C. pulling either of the emergency brake valves (EBV) pull cords located in the customer area or the cab area
    D. all of the above

12. On R62/62A equipment,
    A. all drum switches are in the *THRU* position
    B. drum switches are in the *ON* position at the conductor's position, *OFF* on each end of the train, and *THRU* in between
    C. there are no drum switches on R62/62A equipment
    D. drum switches are set to the *THRU* position

13. On R62/62A equipment, the handbrake is located
    A. beside the customer seat at door panel No. 8
    B. under car at coupler
    C. train operator's cab No. 1
    D. train operator's cab No. 2

14. The MINIMUM air pressure on the duplex air gauge of the R-44 type equipment would be
    A. 80 brake pipe, 110 straight air
    B. 90 main reservoir, 70 brake pipe
    C. 80 straight air, 110 brake pipe
    D. 90 straight air, 130 brake pipe

15. The train operator's console R44 and R46 has a means of braking and propulsion by the use of
    A. master controller and ME-42 brake valve
    B. ME-43 brake valve and master controller
    C. independent brake and throttle
    D. single handle master controller

16. The C/R's operating position on R44 and R46 are located at No.   16.____
    A. 2 end married pair   B. 1 end of a B car
    C. 1 end of an A car   D. 2 end of a B car

17. R44 and R46 cars have sixteen door panels. How many door operators?   17.____
    A. Ten   B. Eight   C. Sixteen   D. Zero

18. For customer safety, between cars R44 and R46, is a device to prevent   18.____
    our customers from boarding between cars. It is known as
    A. safety chain   B. turnstile gate
    C. barrier springs   D. pantograph gates

19. The coupler found on a R44 and R46 is a   19.____
    A. H2A   B. H2C   C. HT4-U93   D. Van Dorm

20. The R46 has a device that keeps the coupler straight on the open ends of   20.____
    the train. It is called
    A. snow brake   B. uncoupling valve
    C. centering device   D. barrier springs

21. Master door controllers are found on R44 and R46   21.____
    A. odd number car of B cars   B. No. 2 end of a B car
    C. No. 1 end of an A car   D. No. 2 end of an A car

22. A train operator, operating a six car R46 would stop his/her train in the   22.____
    station at the _____ marker.
    A. 6 car   B. 10 car   C. 6 car reverse   D. 8 car

23. The side signs on a R44 and R46 are of what type?   23.____
    A. Curtain   B. End sign   C. LCD   D. Motorized

24. The R44 train consisting of A cars and B cars should be made up for   24.____
    service in this order:
    A. ABBAABBA   B. ABBABA   C. BAABBA   D. BBAABABA

25. The adapter can be found on this type of equipment: 25.____
    A. SMEE car   B. R46 car
    C. track geometry car   D. collection train

26. The transverse cab is located on the No.   26.____
    A. 2 end of a married pair   B. 1 end of a B car
    C. 2 end of an A car   D. 1 end of an A car

27. If door panel No. 5 malfunctions, the train operator would cut out   27.____
    A. door operator No. 5   B. door operator No. 4 and No. 5
    C. DC1   D. D8

28. The compressor on a R46 car can be found on which car? 28.____
    A. B car B. C car
    D. SMEE married pair D. A car

29. The odd numbered cars of the R44 are also known as the 29.____
    A. A car B. married pair C. B car D. R68

30. The converter on a R44 can be found on which car? 30.____
    A. A car B. B car C. SMEE car D. R46 B car

31. The R44 and R46 have a device used for uncoupling cars. It is the 31.____
    A. uncoupling valve
    B. electro-pneumatic uncoupling package
    C. centering device
    D. control cut-out switch

32. R68 type equipment has a BCO. It is located near 32.____
    A. No. 3 door panel B. No. 1 door panel
    C. No. 4 door panel D. R68 has no BCO

33. The R68 has how many door operators (door motors)? 33.____
    A. 10 B. 8 C. 16 D. 0

34. The R68 is what type of car? 34.____
    A. Married pair B. Four car unit
    C. Single car D. A car and B car unit

35. The R68 has a transverse cab. It is located on the No. 35.____
    A. 2 end R68 B. 1 end B car C. 2 end A car D. 1 end R68

36. When approaching crosswalks in the yard, the train operator must 36.____
    A. operate at restricted speed with extreme caution through the crosswalk
    B. go through the crosswalk
    C. go through the crosswalk in the third point of power
    D. stop and sound the whistle or horn in a series of short blasts and look in both directions

37. When moving into a Maintenance Shop, the train operator must 37.____
    A. go straight into the shop as soon as the door is opened high enough
    B. take three points of power and go into the shop
    C. before entering, wait for a proceed signal from an employee of the Car Equipment Division at the entrance to the barn
    D. be able to move the cars directly to the block without stopping

38. The FASTEST speed allowed in any yard (unless otherwise posted) is _____ MPH. 38.____
    A. 12 B. 15 C. 10 D. 14

39. While operating in the yard (except R44/R46 type cars) or on storage tracks, the train operator must
    A. sit down while operating
    B. stand where he/she can see best
    C. sit or stand
    D. operate from other than the head end

    39._____

40. An employee who cuts out air brakes on a car must also cut out the
    A. traction motors
    B. BCO
    C. auxiliary air control
    D. brake pipe and straight air cut-out locks

    40._____

KEY (CORRECT ANSWERS)

1. D	11. D	21. C	31. B
2. D	12. C	22. D	32. C
3. D	13. C	23. C	33. C
4. D	14. C	24. A	34. C
5. D	15. D	25. B	35. D
6. C	16. C	26. D	36. D
7. C	17. C	27. A	37. C
8. B	18. C	28. D	38. C
9. D	19. C	29. C	39. B
10. C	20. C	30. A	40. A

TEST 4

DIRECTIONS: Each question or incomplete statement is followed by several suggested answers or completions. Select the one that BEST answers the question or completes the statement. *PRINT THE LETTER OF THE CORRECT ANSWER IN THE SPACE AT THE RIGHT.*

1. When operating in the yard, the train operator must be ready to 1.____
   A. stop one car length, then five feet from standing cars
   B. come to the door of a Maintenance Shop without stopping
   C. make an emergency stop
   D. make a fast stop

2. If brakes are cut out on an end car once a train leaves the terminal, the train 2.____
   A. must be removed from service when it reaches the arriving terminal
   B. can remain in service but the train operator must proceed with caution
   C. must be removed from service at the next station
   D. can remain in service if a road car inspector is on the train

3. If a train operator must cut out the brakes in four cars of a ten-car train, the train 3.____
   A. must be removed from service at the next station
   B. must be removed from service at the arriving terminal
   C. can remain in service if it happens during a midnight tour and a road car inspector is on the train
   D. can remain in service if a road car inspector is on the train

4. If the brakes of a train apply in emergency and the train operator does not know why, the train operator must 4.____
   A. recharge the train and discharge the train at the next station
   B. secure the train and inspect both sides of the trackway
   C. secure the train and inspect both sides of the trackway, as well as a sufficient distance behind the train
   D. recharge the train and proceed but must report the incident to the road car inspector at the arriving terminal

5. Employees who note defects or any unusual conditions that would delay or make unsafe the movement of trains must 5.____
   A. report the defect or condition to the dispatcher upon reach the arriving terminal
   B. inform the road car inspector upon reaching the arriving terminal
   C. determine whether or not the condition really warrants bothering anyone
   D. report it at once to the Control Center Desk Superintendent

6. If power must be removed from the third rail (contact rail) and the emergency telephone does not work and the Control Center Desk Superintendent cannot otherwise be notified, the employee must
   A. report the defect or condition to the dispatcher upon reaching the arriving terminal
   B. turn off the power and be ready to turn the power off again if the power should be restored
   C. not turn off the power until the Transit Police or Fire Department can respond to the scene
   D. turn off the power and go to the nearest station to await the arrival of the Transit Police or Fire Department

6._____

7. In order to remove power immediately, the employee must go to the emergency alarm box at the nearest blue light and
   A. push the button in the emergency alarm box
   B. push the button in the emergency alarm box and call the Power Department
   C. pull down the level fully in the emergency alarm box and call the Control Center Desk Superintendent immediately
   D. push the button firmly and hold it in for a minimum of five seconds

7._____

8. Only the employee who has requested that power be removed may all to have power restored, unless
   A. a senior supervisor of Rapid Transit Operations is on the scene and assumes responsibility
   B. a senior supervisor of the Power Department is on the scene and assumes responsibility
   C. a senior supervisor of any department on the scene can assume responsibility
   D. no one but the employee involved in turning power off may call to have it restored

8._____

9. If the Control Center gives permission for customers to leave a train stopped between stations during an emergency, the train operator must
   A. BCO all of the cars on the train
   B. open the emergency brake valve on every car of the train
   C. cut out all of the motors on the train
   D. open the emergency brake valve and apply sufficient handbrakes

9._____

10. If a customer(s) leaves a train without permission, the train operator must
    A. pull the lever in the emergency alarm box at the station and nearest blue light location or station and immediately notify the Control Center Desk Superintendent
    B. operate the train at *restricted speed with extreme caution* and look for the customer(s)

10._____

C. operate at *restricted speed with extreme caution* and sound the horn in a series of short blasts to warm the customer of the approach of the train
D. secure the train and walk on the trackway. Look for the customer(s) and call to warn the customer(s) that the third rail is alive.

11. If an undesired uncoupling occurs, the train operator must immediately   11._____
    A. pull the power in the emergency alarm box at the nearest blue light and call the Control Center Desk Superintendent
    B. BCO the cars that are uncoupled
    C. re-couple the cars terminal
    D. notify the Control Center Desk Superintendent, then try to recouple and move at *restricted speed with extreme caution* to the next station and discharge customers

12. When a train cannot move under its own power, the train must be secured, the   12._____
    Control Center Desk Superintendent must be notified immediately, and
    A. if the train is on a downgrade, BCO the car so the train can roll into the next station
    B. the following train may couple to it if the same type of coupler and the electric portions are retrieved and locked
    C. the train must be uncoupled in the middle and the good section moved into the station
    D. the customers must immediately be evacuated to the trackway, being careful of the live third rail power

13. Before pushing a train that cannot be moved under its own power, a certain   13._____
    employee must be on the train. That employee is a
    A. Transit Police Officer
    B. road car inspector
    C. signal maintainer and track worker to ensure that the trackway and the signals are safe to proceed on
    D. train service supervisor, superintendent, or other qualified supervisor sent by the Control Center Desk Superintendent

14. When pushing a train that cannot be moved under its own power,   14._____
    A. the road car inspector on the front of the train being pushed will control the power while the train operator on the rear section will control the brakes
    B. the train operator on the front end of the train being pushed will control the brakes. The train operator in the rear section will control the power (master controller)
    C. the train operator on the front end of the train being pushed will operate the master controller and the brakes
    D. a signal maintainer must be on the train to ensure that the signals are working properly

15. When moving cars to couple to other cars in good weather, the train operator must stop at least
    A. five car lengths and 20 feet from standing cars
    B. two car lengths from standing cars
    C. as many times as the train operator deems necessary
    D. two car lengths, then 5 feet, then ten feet, then two feet from the standing cars

16. When moving cars to couple to other cars in bad weather or when the rails are slippery, the train operator must stop at least
    A. five car lengths, two car lengths, then one car length
    B. four car lengths, one car length, and 10 feet
    C. three car lengths, then 50 feet, then 10 feet, then 2 feet from standing cars
    D. four stops that are safe in the train operator's opinion

17. When a train operator's visibility is impaired because of snow, ice, rain, or fog, the train operator must
    A. keep to the train schedule
    B. make sure that under no circumstances will the train be more than five minutes late
    C. not try to keep to the schedule but must run the train slow enough so that it can be stopped within the visible distance
    D. move the train from service

18. If tracks are slippery or weather is bad, what are the safety stops that the train operator must make approaching shop doors and bumping blocks?
    A. One car length and ten feet
    B. Safety stops will be made at the train operator's discretion
    C. Five car lengths, one car length, one-half car length
    D. Three car lengths, then fifty feet, then ten feet

19. Any employee who sees smoke, fire, flood, or an accident on the system must
    A. call the Line Superintendent when the employee arrives at their job site or arriving terminal
    B. immediately report this to the Control Center Desk Superintendent
    C. determine whether or not it is serious enough to call in
    D. call the Track Department or Division of Infrastructure

20. Trains may run on flooded tracks but only with the permission of the Control Center Desk Superintendent and only if the water is
    A. no higher than the top of the wheels on the train
    B. no higher than the tip of the third rail protection board
    C. below the base of the running rail
    D. below the *ball* of the running rail

21. One of the six parts of operating at *restricted speed with extreme caution* is: 21.____
    A. Go no faster than twenty miles per hour
    B. Be prepared to stop a train length from anything visible on the trackway
    C. Be prepared to stop within one-half your range of vision
    D. Be prepared to stop within range of vision

22. Under what conditions is it permissible for a train operator to enter an under-river tunnel when there is a smoke condition? 22.____
    A. If the train operator can stop within one-half the range of vision
    B. If the train operator determines that it is safe to do so
    C. If the conductor walks through the smoke and determines that it is safe to go since the conductor is in charge of trains
    D. Under no condition may a train enter an under-river tunnel from which smoke is coming

23. If a train is in, or stopped, near an accident or derailment, handbrakes must be applied on 23.____
    A. two cars on each end of the train
    B. at least every other car on the train
    C. all of the cars on the train
    D. at least one-third of the cars on a train

24. On a grade, handbrakes MUST be applied on the _____ of the train. 24.____
    A. downgrade end   B. at least every other car
    C. all of the cars   D. at least one-third of the cars

25. If a train has been stopped by an emergency brake application and the brake system cannot be recharged, before leaving the train to check the trouble, the train operator must 25.____
    A. put handbrakes on all cars of the train at all times
    B. put handbrakes on every other car of the train
    C. not put handbrakes on the train in this situation
    D. apply enough handbrakes to keep the train from rolling

26. If customers must be evacuated because of smoke, they should be led to the nearest 26.____
    A. station or emergency exit, regardless of condition
    B. station only
    C. emergency exit only
    D. station or emergency exit unless this would take them into a smoke-filled area. Then they should be led to the nearest station or emergency exit away from the smoke area

27. A train operator must apply the air brakes in emergency and apply sufficient handbrakes on a car or train when
    A. the train stops at the arriving terminal
    B. the train operator makes a station stop on a steep downgrade
    C. a car or train is placed on a siding or storage track, or when enroute it becomes necessary to leave the train, even in a station
    D. the Control Center Desk Superintendent tells the train operator that the train will be behind a red signal for a while

28. A train operator sounds two short blasts of the horn or whistle when
    A. warning other trains to apply brakes immediately
    B. calling for a signal maintainer to respond to a train
    C. giving an answer to any signal
    D. the train crew needs assistance

29. A yellow signal means:
    A. The next signal color ahead will be yellow
    B. The next signal color ahead will be green
    C. Proceed with caution, be prepared to stop
    D. Proceed

30. A blue light means:
    A. Proceed with caution, the next signal is yellow or red
    B. The location of an emergency alarm box, telephone, and fire extinguisher or an emergency telephone only
    C. Proceed, the next signal is green
    D. Stop and call the Control Center Desk superintendent for instructions

31. In order to stop a train, an employee must move the hand, flag, light, or any other object in what manner?
    A. Up and down
    B. To and fro across the track
    C. Diagonally
    D. Parallel to the track

32. In order to give a proceed signal indicating a speed of no more than 5 MPH, an employee must move the hand, flag, or light in what manner?
    A. Up and down
    B. To and fro across the track
    C. Horizontally
    D. Hold the hand or a white light away from the body, in a steady position

33. A train operator must have a properly functioning flashlight in their personal possession
    A. only while operating a train
    B. only while operating a train or waiting for a lay-up
    C. everywhere, except while working in an outside yard during the daytime
    D. while on duty

34. Before releasing the handbrakes on a train, the train operator must   34.____
    A. BCO all of the cars
    B. fully charge the air brake system and apply the brakes in emergency
    C. take one point of power and see if the train rolls
    D. open an emergency brake valve at the conductor's position

35. Express trains running on local tracks will make only express stops unless   35.____
    crews are told otherwise. The exception is when
    A. trains are running ahead of schedule
    B. trains are running behind schedule
    C. it is necessary to re-route express trains to local tracks due to cold
       weather plans
    D. trains are running on a headway of ten minutes or more

36. When going to the left or right over a switch and unless otherwise posted, a   36.____
    train operator can go no faster than _____ MPH.
    A. 10   B. 12   C. 15   D. 20

37. If a customer train must be run from other than the head end, on the road, the   37.____
    method of communication should be
    A. buzzer or horn signals
    B. light or hand signals
    C. sound-powered telephone or radio
    D. horn or light signals

38. Two long buzzer sounds mean: 38.____
    A. Signal for train operator to call for a road car inspector
    B. Signal for conductor to come to train operator's cab
    C. Proceed
    D. An answer to any signal

39. Two short buzzer sounds mean: 39.____
    A. An answer to any signal
    B. Proceed
    C. Stop
    D. Signal for conductor to come to train operator's cab

40. A long, short, long, short buzzer sound means: 40.____
    A. An answer to any signal
    B. Stop
    C. Signal for the train operator to sound the train horn or whistle for
       assistance
    D. Proceed slowly

KEY (CORRECT ANSWERS)

1.	C	11.	D	21.	C	31.	B
2.	C	12.	B	22.	D	32.	D
3.	A	13.	D	23.	C	33.	D
4.	C	14.	B	24.	A	34.	B
5.	D	15.	D	25.	D	35.	C
6.	B	16.	C	26.	D	36.	A
7.	C	17.	C	27.	C	37.	C
8.	A	18.	D	28.	C	38.	C
9.	D	19.	B	29.	C	39.	A
10.	A	20.	D	30.	B	40.	C

TEST 5

DIRECTIONS: Each question or incomplete statement is followed by several suggested answers or completions. Select the one that BEST answers the question or completes the statement. *PRINT THE LETTER OF THE CORRECT ANSWER IN THE SPACE AT THE RIGHT.*

1. A train operator sounds one long and one short, one long and one short blast of the horn or whistle when   1.____
    A. requesting a road car inspector
    B. the train crew needs assistance
    C. answering any signal
    D. requesting the tower operator or hand switcher for route or signal

2. A train operator sounds two long blasts of the horn or whistle on the train when   2.____
    A. requesting a road car inspector
    B. the train crew needs assistance
    C. passing caution lights or flagging to warn the flagger of the approach of a train
    D. requesting a tower operator or hand switcher for the route or signal

3. Five short buzzer sounds mean: 3.____
    A. Proceed at no more than five miles per hour
    B. An answer to any signal
    C. Signal for train operator to sound horn or whistle for assistance
    D. Signal for conductor to come to the train operator's cab

4. The FASTEST speed that a train operator can operate inside the shop is _____ MPH.   4.____
    A. 5   B. 8   C. 10   D. 15

5. If a train operator stops in the shop and loses power, the employee who must apply a 600 volt trolley to the car or cars would be a   5.____
    A. train operator
    B. train service supervisor
    C. power maintainer
    D. Division of Car Equipment employee

6. A train operator can key-by a(n) _____ signal.   6.____
    A. automatic   B. dwarf   C. marker   D. bumper

7. The safety stops that a train operator must make when approaching standing cars in a barn are: 7.____
    A. One car length, then ten feet
    B. Fifty feet, then ten feet
    C. Two car lengths, then one car length
    D. Three-car lengths, then fifty feet, then ten feet, and two feet

8. Before making an unplanned wrong rail move, the train operator must
   A. walk the tracks ahead to make sure that no employees are working on the tracks
   B. go no faster than twenty miles per hour
   C. be instructed to do so by the Control Center Desk Superintendent
   D. make sure not to operate with more than three points of power

9. A train operator cannot key-by a(n) _____ SIGNAL.
   A. automatic   B. grade time   C. station time   D. home

10. After stopping the train, a train operator is given permission to move past a red automatic signal with a "K" sign. He/She must
    A. pull up to the signal, stop, and wait for the stop arm to go down
    B. proceed at no faster than 15 MPH. The stop arm will go down automatically.
    C. secure the train and go down on the tracks to hook down the stop arm
    D. pull up to the signal and stop, use the automatic stop arm release lever, button or special key to make the automatic stop arm go down

11. If a signal is unlit, the train operator must
    A. proceed past the signal, being prepared to stop within the range of vision
    B. stop and report immediately by radio to the Control Center Desk Superintendent
    C. stop, then proceed past the signal no faster than 15 MPH
    D. observe that the automatic stop arm is down, then proceed past the signal

12. What type of a stop arm can NEVER go down?
    A. Automatic stop arm
    B. Stop arm associated with an approach signal
    C. Fixed stop
    D. Stop arm associated with a grade time signal

13. What device is placed across the rail to prevent a train from overrunning the end of the track?
    A. A bumper block
    B. An automatic stop arm hook
    C. Automatic stop arm
    D. Semi-automatic stop arm

14. A handbrake is located at which end of the car?
    A. No. 1 end
    B. No. 2 end
    C. Center excess end
    D. It is located in the middle of the car

15. The purpose of a BCO is to
    A. remove the handbrake feature from the car
    B. removed the air brake feature from the car
    C. remove the dynamic brake feature from the car
    D. add the dynamic brake feature to the car

16. If a train operator accepts a call-on at a home signal, the train operator will proceed
    A. no faster than 12 MPH
    B. no faster than 15 MPH
    C. at *restricted speed with extreme caution*
    D. at a speed where he/she can stop within range of vision

17. If the automatic stop arm of a home signal does not go down after the train operator operates the lever or button twice (a call-on has been displayed), he/she must
    A. keep pressing the button or lever until the stop arm goes down
    B. hook the stop arm down and proceed
    C. call and receive orders from the Control Center Desk Superintendent
    D. wait until the signal changes to proceed

18. If a train operator sees a yellow sign with 20 Miles on it, and also sees a set of caution lights or flags on the track, at what speed must he/she go?
    A. No faster than 20 MPH
    B. Fast enough to get to the arriving terminal on time
    C. Go at *restricted speed with extreme caution* and sound two long blasts of the horn or whistle
    D. There is no speed restriction. The sign indicated how far the train has traveled from the leaving terminal.

19. If a train goes past a fixed signal indicating red, what device causes an emergency application of the air brakes?
    A. Automatic stop
    B. BCO
    C. Dynamic brake
    D. Handbrake

20. The train operator's indication is
    A. the buzzer signal that tells the train operator to move the train on the trackway
    B. the horn signal to alert employee that a train is approaching
    C. a sequence of radio signals to the train operator indicating that he/she must slow the train speed
    D. the light in the train operator's cab that illuminates when all side doors are close and locked

21. A guard light is a light
    A. that tells the train operator that the front storm door is closed and locked
    B. that tells the train operator that the rear storm door is closed and locked
    C. on a car that illuminates if any one door or doors are not properly closed and locked on that car
    D. tells the train operator and conductor that a handbrake is applied somewhere on the train

22. A door fault light is a light
    A. that illuminates when the end storm door is not properly closed and locked
    B. which illuminates if that door (passenger door on the side of the train) is not properly closed and locked
    C. which illuminates when the front storm door is not properly closed or locked
    D. that goes dark when the doors are opened

23. A propulsion fault light is an amber light on the side of the car that illuminates when
    A. the propulsion system on that car has been automatically disconnected (dead motors)
    B. the train starts to move
    C. the motors in that car continue to take power after the train operator has shut power off
    D. the dynamic brakes are working

24. A conductor's indication is a
    A. sequence of radio signals to the conductor to let him/her know the train is ready to move
    B. light that tells the conductor that the rear storm door is unlocked
    C. light that tells the conductor that a handbrake is applied somewhere on the train
    D. light or lights at the conductor's operating position that illuminates when all doors are closed and locked, and when the zone or drum switches are set correctly

25. A train operator must have indication and what signal from the conductor before starting a train carrying customers from a terminal?
    A. Two long buzzer signals
    B. The conductor turns the car body lights off and on
    C. One long buzzer signal
    D. Two long blasts of the horn or whistle

26. A train makes an emergency stop and the train operator locates and corrects the problem. After the train recharges, the train operator's indication illuminates. What signal must the train operator receive from the conductor before starting the train?
    A. Two long blasts of the horn or whistle
    B. The conductor turns the car body lights off and on
    C. One long buzzer signal
    D. Two long buzzer signals

27. If both the train operator and conductor lose indication while moving, the train operator must
    A. slow down to *restricted speed with extreme caution* to the next station
    B. operate in service but report the problem at the arriving terminal
    C. stop the train, then call the Control Center and investigate
    D. immediately slow down to 20 MPH or less

28. If a side door or doors open when the train is starting to move out of the station, the train operator must
    A. operate no faster than 10 MPH to the terminal
    B. stop the train, call the Control Center, make sure that no one fell to the trackway, and take the train out of service immediately
    C. operate to the next station, then investigate
    D. investigate and overcome the problem, then operate to the arriving terminal where the train must be removed from service

29. If the train operator's indication fails to work after the train has left the terminal in customer service, the train operator
    A. must take the train out of service
    B. may keep the train in service as long as the conductor has indication in both zones
    C. should operate at *restricted speed with extreme caution*
    D. can remain in service but operate prepared to make a fast stop

30. A red signal, in a time controlled area, that also displays a lunar white aspect means
    A. the signal may be cleared by a train approaching said signal at a predetermined speed
    B. stop and call the Control Center Desk Superintendent
    C. stop and operate the automatic stop manual release lever
    D. stop, secure the train, and find a telephone to call the local tower

31. There is a fixed signal, located within the station limits at a terminal, which illuminates to green with the sound of a bell going off at the same time. It is called a _____ signal.
    A. gap filler
    B. station holding
    C. train starting
    D. train order

32. A fixed signal located within the station limits, when illuminated, the conductor must keep the train doors open. The color of this signal is
    A. red   B. green   C. blue   D. yellow

33. What codes would a train operator use, respectively, if he/she wanted to notify the Control Center that their train derailed in a water condition?
    A. 12-4, 12-8   B. 12-3, 12-6   C. 12-6, 12-3   D. 122, 12-8

34. What are the following military times in regular time: 1320 hours, 2350 hours, 0315 hours?
    A. 1:20 AM, 3:50 PM, 3:15 AM
    B. 3:20 AM, 2:50 PM, 3:15 PM
    C. 1:32 PM, 2:35 PM, 10:15 AM
    D. 1:20 PM, 11:50 PM, 3:15 AM

35. What is the FIRST thing that an employee must do before crossing any track?
    A. An employee must contact both of the running rails.
    B. An employee must make contact with the third rail and one of the running rails.
    C. Listen for the sound of a train, then step into the track.
    D. Look and listen in both directions before entering upon any track.

36. Contact rail (third rail) jumpers are used when a(n)
    A. employee must contact both of the running rails
    B. employee must make contact with the third rail and one of the running rails
    C. car or train becomes stalled in a contact rail gap (loses third rail power)
    D. car or train needs to be jumped to the signal rail

37. The MAXIMUM speed allowed for a work train on straight track is _____ MPH.
    A. 15   B. 20   C. 25   D. 30

38. The main reason for NOT operating a train for an extended period of time in the switching position is to
    A. prevent damage to the car equipment
    B. conserve power
    C. prevent accidents
    D. allow the train to operate automatically

39. The LEAST likely result of a train passing an automatic signal whose aspect is red is
    A. damage to the car equipment
    B. injuries to the passengers
    C. a delay in train service
    D. damage to the signal's automatic stop arm

40. All car equipment failures must be reported by the motorman
    A. to the road car inspector
    B. to the command center
    C. on the train register sheet
    D. on the car defect sheet

KEY (CORRECT ANSWERS)

1.	B	11.	B	21.	C	31.	C
2.	C	12.	C	22.	B	32.	D
3.	D	13.	A	23.	A	33.	C
4.	A	14.	A	24.	D	34.	D
5.	D	15.	B	25.	A	35.	D
6.	A	16.	C	26.	D	36.	C
7.	D	17.	C	27.	C	37.	C
8.	C	18.	C	28.	B	38.	A
9.	D	19.	A	29.	B	39.	D
10.	D	20.	D	30.	A	40.	D

EXAMINATION SECTION
TEST 1

DIRECTIONS: Each question or incomplete statement is followed by several suggested answers or completions. Select the one that BEST answers the question or completes the statement. *PRINT THE LETTER OF THE CORRECT ANSWER IN THE SPACE AT THE RIGHT.*

1. A "1" displayed on the heat and ventilation board at a terminal during the winter season means that
    A. one point of heat should be on in each car
    B. one window should be open on each side of each car
    C. the car ventilators are to be opened to the number one position
    D. one heat switch should be closed on each car

    1.____

2. In an attempt to provide a more comfortable ride for the subway passengers, the Transit Authority has installed
    A. automatic coupling
    B. welded rail joints
    C. wider car seats
    D. dynamic braking

    2.____

3. A train operator who has just made a station stop on level track and is waiting for his indication light should have his brake valve handle in
    A. release
    B. lap
    C. electric holding
    D. service

    3.____

4. One conductor on a ten-car train is all that is required by the latest rules of the Transit Authority. The MAIN reason for reducing the number of conductors on such a train is because
    A. since the last fare increase there are less people riding the subways
    B. door controls have been greatly improved
    C. most of the stations on the system have been extended to accommodate ten-car trains
    D. operating costs can be reduced with safety

    4.____

5. The Transit Authority has installed bright running lights on subway cars. Of the following, the MAIN objection to such lights is that they
    A. use too much electricity
    B. can "blind" an employee standing alongside the subway track
    C. are difficult and costly to maintain
    D. distract a train operator from paying strict attention to track signals

    5.____

6. Of the following, the MOST probable reason for limiting the speed of trains in under-river tunnels is that
    A. the trains cannot safely maintain high speed for long distances
    B. passengers may be afraid that the train will go off the track
    C. there is limited clearance in such tunnels
    D. at slower speeds annoying air pressure on the ears is eliminated

    6.____

7. If a train operator, about to start out from a terminal, finds that he cannot move his controller handle from the OFF position, he should first check if the
   A. third rail is alive
   B. duplex air gauge shows proper pressures
   C. brakes have had time to release
   D. reverser has been moved to the forward position

7.____

8. An INCORRECT statement to make about a subway car is that it has
   A. two train operator's operating cabs
   B. four contact shoes
   C. four trip cocks
   D. two conductor's valves

8.____

9. If it is necessary to cut out a door that is stuck open on a revenue train stopped at a station, the FIRST step should be to
   A. force the door closed with a contact shoe slipper
   B. close the cut-out cock on the air line to the door engine
   C. operate the emergency door device
   D. turn the snap switch that controls the door engine to the OFF position

9.____

10. If a train operator is informed that there is smoke coming out from under his train which is making a regular station stop, he should immediately
    A. notify his conductor   B. call the transit police
    C. check to determine the cause   D. have the power shut off

10.____

11. The position to which the master controller handle has been moved by the train operator determines the
    A. maximum speed to which the train may accelerate
    B. number of motors in use
    C. final rate of acceleration
    D. initial rate of acceleration

11.____

12. When operating "pneumatically," the train operator of a ten-car train must exercise greater caution than the train operator of a six-car train because, under this condition of operation, the longer train has
    A. slower acting brakes   B. less braking power
    C. quicker acting brakes   D. more braking power

12.____

Questions 13-17.

DIRECTIONS: Questions 13 through 17 are based on the rule immediately preceding each item. Be sure to consider only the information given in the rule which immediately precedes the item.

RULE: A train must not proceed on a hand signal as against fixed signal indications until the train operator is fully informed of the situation, and only after the train has come to a stop.

13. The probable reason for this rule is that a
    A. fixed signal gives all possible information
    B. hand signal is never valid
    C. hand signal may be incomplete or misunderstood
    D. fixed signal always indicates correctly

13._____

RULE: Any signal imperfectly displayed, or the absence of a signal where a signal is usually shown, must be regarded as the most restrictive indication that can be given by that signal.

14. One justification for this rule is that
    A. a train operator may mistake the intended indication
    B. imperfectly displayed signals always display their most restrictive aspects
    C. the most restrictive indication is generally proceed with caution
    D. in this way delay is reduced to a minimum

14._____

RULE: Train operators must approach all STOP signals, trains ahead, junctions, and terminals with train under full control.

15. Having the train under full control means MOST NEARLY
    A. slowing your train down to 10 M.P.H. and holding that speed
    B. operating your train so that you can stop it smoothly within your range of vision
    C. standing with both your hands on the controls
    D. having your reverser forward, master controller off, and brake handle in release

15._____

RULE: Train operators must be careful not to overrun station platforms. Should this happen, however, they must give prescribed whistle signal and wait for the prescribed signal from conductor before proceeding. Under no circumstances will train operators back train if they have overrun station platform.

16. The MOST likely reason for this rule is based on the fact that
    A. the train passengers may become panicky
    B. passengers on the platform may be injured
    C. the train operator of the following train may be confused
    D. the train operator cannot see conditions at the other end of the train

16._____

RULE: Before coupling cars, train operators must see that the brake is set up on the section to which coupling is to be made. When making coupling on grade, they must move cars upgrade.

17. The principle safety feature realized by coupling upgrade is that the
    A. hand brakes do not have to be set up on the stationary section before coupling
    B. impact is less
    C. coupler on the stationary section is centered because it hangs downgrade
    D. stationary cars cannot accidentally roll away if the coupling fails to make

18. Train operators generally know the points at which coasting is required under normal conditions by
    A. judgment gained through experience
    B. bulletins posted at their home terminals
    C. signs along the route
    D. verbal instructions from the train operator instructor

19. Warm weather would probably cause more
    A. door trouble due to moisture in the air lines
    B. hot armature bearings
    C. brake shoe wear
    D. brake pipe leakage

20. A candidate for train operator who has passed the written test but still has to pass the performance test would probably learn most about train operation from
    A. attending lectures on operation at the school
    B. studying printed instruction sheets for guidance of train operators
    C. asking questions of veteran train operators
    D. handling the equipment whenever possible

21. All new appointees in the transit system are given a booklet with a detailed printed schedule of working conditions for that particular title. The PRINCIPAL reason for being given this booklet is that this procedure
    A. equalizes work loads
    B. prevents grievances
    C. standardizes the conditions of employment
    D. minimizes the necessity for overtime work

22. The transit employee chiefly responsible for correct display of front end destination signs on a train before leaving the terminal is the
    A. conductor   B. platformman
    C. train operator   D. dispatcher

23. The MOST important feature of a good train air brake system is
    A. ability to stop a train smoothly in a short distance
    B. simplicity of maintenance
    C. simplicity of operation
    D. ability to stop the train abruptly

23.____

24. Before changing ends at a terminal, the train operator must make a brake pipe reduction of
    A. 10 lbs.   B. 20 lbs.   C. 30 lbs.   D. full emergency

24.____

25. A train operator should know that a "slow train" means a
    A. train which brakes slowly
    B. train which accelerates slowly
    C. train whose doors open slowly
    D. rerouted express on the local track

25.____

26. If a brake pipe rupture occurs when a train is coming to a stop, the train operator will
    A. have no control of the brakes
    B. be able to stop his train with a service application
    C. have to apply the hand brakes to stop the train
    D. be able to make a normal stop

26.____

27. If the power supply for the third rail in the subway fails,
    A. all car lights will be dark
    B. train operator's indication lights will become inoperative
    C. air compressors on cars will not operate
    D. electro-pneumatic brakes will be inoperative

27.____

Questions 28-36.

DIRECTIONS: Questions 28 through 36, inclusive in Column I, are train operating situations, each of which is restricted to a maximum of one of the operating speeds listed in Column II. For each situation in Column I, select the appropriate maximum operating speed from Column II. Print the letter of your selected operating speed in the numbered space at the right. (Assume normal conditions with no speed signs.)

	Column I	Column II	
28.	On straight yard tracks	A. Series	28.____
		B. Slowly	
29.	Entering a terminal	C. 10 MPH	29.____
		D. 25 MPH	
30.	In river tubes	E. 20 MPH	30.____
		F. 25 MPH	
31.	Over diverging routes	G. 30 MPH	31.____
		H. 35 MPH	
32.	Entering an inspection shed		32.____
33.	Skipping a station		33.____
34.	Rounding a sharp curve in a yard		34.____
35.	Immediate resumption of service after stopping for two minutes on Veteran's Day		35.____
36.	Passing through an area covered by three yellow lanterns suspended alongside the track		36.____

37. A train operator should know that the automatic stop mechanisms used on the subway system are designed so that in case of signal power failure the stop arms will automatically move to the tripping position even though the locks ahead are clear. This is done because
    A. it is easier to hook a stop arm down than to hold it up
    B. it is safer to have the stop arms in the tripping position when signal power fails
    C. it is impossible to move trains at such a time
    D. when signal power fails, the subway lighting system also goes out

37.____

38. In reference to subway flagging procedure, an entirely correct statement is that
    A. "Stop" signs may not be given with either a yellow or a white light
    B. at any time, if yellow lanterns are displayed, there is always a flagman nearby
    C. lights set up in a flagging arrangement on a station platform must not be left unattended
    D. flagmen are always stationed directly adjacent to the nearest point of work or obstruction

38._____

39. Suppose your conductor was told by an excited passenger that, just before the train entered the portal which is about midway between the last station and the one at which you are stopped, a window in one of the cars was shattered by a stone. The BEST of the following sequences of action for the conductor to follow is to
    A. open the conductor's valve, signal the train operator to whistle for a police officer, proceed to the broken window and take appropriate action
    B. leave the doors open, follow the passenger back to the broken window, take down names of witnesses and get the story
    C. signal the train operator to whistle for a police officer, turn in an emergency alarm, call the superintendent
    D. open the conductor's valve, proceed immediately to the broken window, offer first aid to those who have been cut

39._____

40. Many new types of interlocking home signals are equipped with route request buttons. These buttons are to be operated by the train operator when the home signal is at danger and no call-on is displayed, or when improper route is displayed. When the button is operated, a light goes on over the button to show the train operator's request has registered in the tower. The tower operator acknowledges the request by either changing the route or canceling the light over the route request buttons. If a train operator pulls up to a signal indicating a wrong route and operates the route request button and receives no acknowledgment from the tower operator, it would be improper for the train operator to
    A. whistle for the signal maintainer
    B. secure his train and call the superintendent
    C. follow up his unanswered request to the tower operator with the appropriate whistle blast
    D. accept the route that is set up and report it later at the nearest dispatcher's office

40._____

41. The MOST likely reason for the installation of route request buttons as described in Question 40 is to
    A. increase the train operator's responsibility
    B. keep the tower operator alert
    C. speed up service
    D. improve working conditions

41._____

42. An express train requires six minutes to make the run between two stations which are three and one-half miles apart. The average speed of the train for this run is _____ MPH.
    A. 21 B. 28 C. 35 D. 42

43. Power from the storage battery is used to operate the
    A. air compressor
    B. train whistle
    C. train operator's indication light
    D. side destination sign lights

44. The train operator should first be aware that the electric brake has failed and they are operating pneumatically when they
    A. notice the delay in the initial brake application
    B. feels the reduced braking effort
    C. makes the initial release
    D. finally stops the train

45. During rush hours in particular, if train operators make accurate stops at the stop markers, the one who will derive the greatest benefit is the
    A. conductor, for he will have a better view of conditions on the platform
    B. platform man who will be standing where the crowd will gather
    C. train operator, in his realization that he is operating almost perfectly
    D. passenger who was unable to get on the preceding train, for he will now be standing near a door

46. Train operators are continually cautioned that, if they have to hook down the automatic stop arm in order to pass an automatic signal, they must release the stop arm again immediately after the train has passed, unless okayed by the signal maintainer or other qualified employee. The MAIN reason for releasing the stop arm again is
    A. so that the signal head will light up once more
    B. to permit normal operation of all signals in the area
    C. to give protection to a following train
    D. to minimize train delays

47. If the train whistle becomes inoperative enroute, the train operator should
    A. proceed cautiously and report the condition at the first opportunity
    B. have the conductor blow the whistle in the cab of his car
    C. operate from the second car
    D. stop immediately and call the control center for orders

48. If the motors on a car continue to take power when the master controller is in the OFF position, the train operator should
    A. apply the brakes in emergency
    B. close the control switch
    C. reset the line switch
    D. put on some hand brakes

49. Of the following, the LEAST likely reason for ordering a train out of service would be a
    A. pair of flat wheels
    B. defective brake valve in head cab
    C. open in the battery control line
    D. car lit by emergency lights only

50. The force necessary to apply the brakes on a subway car is supplied by the
    A. air compressors
    B. batteries
    C. brake springs
    D. brake rigging

KEY (CORRECT ANSWERS)

1.	A	11.	A	21.	C	31.	C	41.	C
2.	B	12.	A	22.	C	32.	B	42.	C
3.	A	13.	C	23.	A	33.	D	43.	C
4.	D	14.	A	24.	D	34.	C	44.	A
5.	B	15.	B	25.	B	35.	A	45.	D
6.	B	16.	D	26.	A	36.	C	46.	C
7.	D	17.	D	27.	C	37.	B	47.	A
8.	C	18.	C	28.	A	38.	C	48.	A
9.	B	19.	B	29.	D	39.	A	49.	D
10.	C	20.	D	30.	H	40.	D	50.	A

TEST 2

DIRECTIONS: Each question or incomplete statement is followed by several suggested answers or completions. Select the one that BEST answers the question or completes the statement. *PRINT THE LETTER OF THE CORRECT ANSWER IN THE SPACE AT THE RIGHT.*

Questions 1-5.

DIRECTIONS: Questions 1 through 5, inclusive, are based on the accident described below. Read this description carefully before answering these questions.

ACCIDENT

At 11 A.M. on a Wednesday, the last two cars of a ten-car southbound express train were derailed when taking the crossover between the two southbound tracks of a four-track subway line. There were no posted speed restrictions at the crossover. There were only minor injuries to passengers in the last three cars, and the following train closed up to the derailed train and took off all the passengers. The train operator of the derailed train, on orders from the train service supervisor, was sent to the nearest transit M.A.C. for examination.

1. It can logically be assumed that traffic was considerably delayed on 1.____
    A. one track   B. two tracks   C. three tracks   D. four tracks

2. The MOST probable reason for sending the train operator to have an examination was 2.____
    A. to detect possible injuries
    B. to ensure the train operator was not impaired
    C. for a record in case of lawsuits by injured passengers
    D. to meet the requirements of Workmen's Compensation

3. The MOST important safety precaution which should have been taken before removing passengers from the derailed train was to 3.____
    A. place the brakes of the following train in emergency and set up a hand brake
    B. place the brakes of the disabled train in emergency and set up a hand brake
    C. "kill" the third rails
    D. send the conductor of the following train back to act as a flagman

4. It can be assumed that the first realization the train operator had that something was wrong was the 4.____
    A. train operator's indication light going dark
    B. conductor's buzzer signal
    C. loss of speed
    D. first signal immediately in front of the train changing to red

5. The MOST probable cause of the derailment was
   A. an inexperienced train operator
   B. flat wheels
   C. a badly worn crossover
   D. excessive speed

6. The force necessary to release the applied brakes on a subway car is supplied by the
   A. air compressors
   B. batteries
   C. brake springs
   D. brake rigging

7. Of the following actions of train operators, the one which would be considered a violation of rules is for them to
   A. coast as instructed when operation is normal
   B. stop the train and descend to extinguish a small fire
   C. "take a stretch" after coupling cars together to make up a train
   D. use switching position on the master controller as a running position

8. Conductors are required to carry Transit Authority mail from one station to another when so requested by a
   A. dispatcher
   B. transit officer
   C. railroad clerk
   D. signal foreman

9. Trains are operated in both directions on a single track in under-river tunnels whenever certain kinds of work must be done, alternate trains running in opposite directions. If the running time between the two towers at the ends of a certain tunnel is 4½ minutes, the MINIMUM headway in one direction when such single-tracking is operated is nearest to _____ minutes.
   A. 5
   B. 10
   C. 13½
   D. 15

10. When cars are coupled, they should be brought together from a few feet apart at a speed of about 1.5 feet per second. This speed is MOST NEARLY equal to _____ MPH.
    A. ½
    B. ¾
    C. 1
    D. 1¼

11. It is most important that a train operator, who tripped and fell on the track as he was walking in from a yard lead, give complete details of the accident on the accident report because this will
    A. cause the train operator to be more careful in the future
    B. keep fellow workers advised of any hazardous working conditions
    C. help the Transit Authority in the defense of any false compensation claims
    D. provide information to help avoid future accidents

12. If the master controller handle of a train standing in a station is moved to an ON position when the black arrow of the duplex gauge indicates 55 pounds, the train will
    A. remain stationary
    B. accelerate too slowly
    C. accelerate normally
    D. accelerate too rapidly

13. A recent bulletin stated that the conductors are not allowing enough time for passengers to detrain and entrain before closing the doors. The MOST serious result of such action is that the
    A. trains will run ahead of schedule
    B. passengers getting on may have the door closed in their faces
    C. passengers may be hurt
    D. passengers may not get off the train in time and have to rise past station

13._____

14. After a brake application, if the brake valve is placed in electric holding when the electric brake is not cut in, the result will be that the brakes will
    A. be inoperative
    B. go into emergency
    C. remain applied
    D. release

14._____

15. Of the following actions, the one which is LEAST likely to cause flat wheels is for a train operator to
    A. exceed the allowable speed on a curve
    B. operate the controller before hand brakes are fully released
    C. make hard stops
    D. run with dragging brakes

15._____

16. Before using a shoe paddle, an important precaution for train operators to take is to make certain that
    A. the third rail is dead
    B. the paddle is not cracked
    C. the conductor is on the track with the train operator
    D. they are standing on a tie

16._____

17. It is permissible for a train operator to reverse the car motors in order to prevent
    A. a collision
    B. flat wheels
    C. a derailment
    D. bridging a third rail gap

17._____

18. The BEST procedure for operating a passenger train past a number of successive grade time signals is to
    A. hold speed to a uniform value so that each signal clears when the train is about halfway through the block
    B. slow down at the beginning of each block so that the signal clears when the train is about halfway through the block, then apply power
    C. hold speed as nearly constant as possible so that each signal clears a short distance ahead of the train
    D. pick up speed at the entrance to each block, then slow down about halfway through, so that the signal clears a short distance ahead of the train

18._____

19. Two lamps are used in the train operator's indication light fixture. The MOST probable reason for this practice is in order to
    A. reduce the current in the circuit
    B. retain an indication if one of the lamps burn out
    C. reduce the voltage on each lamp
    D. increase the brightness of the indication

20. Hand brakes should be set up on a train when the
    A. third rail power is likely to be off for some time
    B. train has stopped on a grade at a home signal indicating "stop and stay"
    C. train operator is changing ends at a terminal
    D. electric brake is cut out

21. The reset relay on a subway train is used to reset the _____ relay.
    A. emergency light   B. battery
    C. limit   D. overload

22. If a car is laid up on a yard track, with the air brakes applied and the air compressor cut out of service, the brake would "creep off" most quickly by a slow leak in the
    A. brake pipe   B. brake cylinder
    C. coupler hose   D. main reservoir

23. Three principal fixed signal indications are PROCEED, PROCEED WITH CAUTION, and STOP. The PROCEED WITH CAUTION indication means MOST NEARLY
    A. go at not over 15 miles per hour
    B. go slow so as to be able to stop within range of vision
    C. no need to slow down before reaching the next signal
    D. go at normal speed for the particular track condition

24. When train operators read a bulletin order stating that a certain track will be operated as an "absolute block" between two specified points, they should know that on this particular track
    A. only one train at a time may be between the specified points
    B. trains will proceed on hand signals only
    C. only one direction of traffic will be allowed
    D. alternate trains will run in opposite directions

25. At transfer points, it is especially desirable that trains make "meets"
    A. if there is a temporary tie-up in service
    B. at all times
    C. during rush hours
    D. late at night

26. A round trip time between two terminals, not including layover time, is one hour. A train due to arrive at one terminal at 10:20 should leave the other terminal at
    A. 9:05   B. 9:20   C. 9:35   D. 9:50

27. On approaching a location where employees are working on the tracks in the subway, a train operator observes a yellow lantern waved up and down. This indicates that the train operator should
    A. expect to find another group of workers a short distance beyond the yellow lantern
    B. expect to find a green lantern a train length past the yellow lantern
    C. resume normal operation after passing the yellow lantern
    D. bring his train to a stop before reaching the yellow lantern

28. There is no rapid transit tunnel of the N.Y.C.T.A. under the East River at _____ Street.
    A. 14th
    B. 34th
    C. 42nd
    D. 60th

29. Of the following, the MOST important element of good rapid transit service today is the
    A. fluorescent lighting in the cars and on the stations
    B. dynamic braking system on all the new cars
    C. ability of the railroad personnel to keep the trains on schedule
    D. modern design of the new cars which gives added riding comfort

30. A person standing next to the tracks facing an oncoming train with their left arm extended straight out and away from their body is asking the approaching train operator to
    A. give an acknowledgment on the train horn that the approaching train sees there are employees on or near the track
    B. approach standing person at no more than 5 MPH for the purpose of picking them up or receiving instructions
    C. acknowledge that the next station stop has workers on the track and the train operator needs to allow them time to clear-up
    D. informing the approaching train operator per rules that there may be signals out ahead due to work being performed

KEY (CORRECT ANSWERS)

1.	B	11.	D	21.	D
2.	B	12.	A	22.	B
3.	A	13.	C	23.	B
4.	C	14.	D	24.	A
5.	D	15.	A	25.	D
6.	C	16.	B	26.	D
7.	D	17.	A	27.	A
8.	A	18.	C	28.	B
9.	B	19.	B	29.	C
10.	C	20.	A	30.	B

EXAMINATION SECTION
TEST 1

DIRECTIONS: Each question or incomplete statement is followed by several suggested answers or completions. Select the one that BEST answers the question or completes the statement. *PRINT THE LETTER OF THE CORRECT ANSWER IN THE SPACE AT THE RIGHT.*

1. There is a rapid transit tunnel of the N.Y.C.T.A. under the East River at _____ Street.
   A. 34th   B. 23rd   C. 14th   D. Canal

   1.____

2. The accepted procedure used in helping to release hand brakes which will not release easily is to first
   A. tighten the hand brakes a little more and then release them
   B. notch the controller up one point and return immediately
   C. make a light service application
   D. apply the air brakes in emergency

   2.____

3. It is generally true that the principal cause of most accidents is
   A. defective equipment   B. fatigue
   C. carelessness   D. physical disability

   3.____

4. An incorrect statement to make about a subway cat is that it has only two
   A. trip cocks   B. uncoupling valves
   C. brake valves   D. air gauges

   4.____

5. If a car develops a grounded shoe beam, the train operator should FIRST
   A. signal for a car inspector
   B. break off the shoe
   C. remove the shoe fuse
   D. pull the nearest emergency alarm box

   5.____

6. The brake system of a train is recharged when the ME-23 brake valve is in
   A. release   B. lap   C. service   D. emergency

   6.____

7. The equalizing piston is MOST closely associated with the
   A. E-1 safety valve   B. feed valve
   C. brake cylinder   D. ME-23 brake valve

   7.____

8. If the brakes "creep on," the train operator could reasonably suspect that somewhere on the train there is a
   A. feed valve which is not properly adjusted
   B. leaky brake cylinder
   C. slack adjuster with insufficient slack
   D. leaky trip cock

   8.____

9. When making up trains, the practice of "taking a stretch" is to test the
   A. motors
   B. hand brakes
   C. couplers
   D. safety gates

10. When making up trains in a yard in very cold weather, the train operator could expect to find trouble with the
    A. couplers
    B. doors
    C. motors
    D. axles

11. If the batteries on a train are dead, it will still be possible to
    A. communicate by buzzer signal
    B. operate the doors normally
    C. apply the air brakes
    D. have train operator's indication lights

12. If train operators notice that their train stops beyond the usual spot when they make a normal brake application in making a station stop, they should suspect a defect in the
    A. electric brake
    B. compressors
    C. controller
    D. variable load valves

13. If a train is tripped while running at about 20 MPH, the MOST likely damage to the equipment would be
    A. locked brakes
    B. flat wheels
    C. hot journal boxes
    D. worn brake shoes

14. If seven eight-car trains and eight ten-car trains pass a point on a certain track in one hour, the average headway on that track is _____ minutes.
    A. 3
    B. 4
    C. 5
    D. 6

15. When cars are coupled, they should be brought together from a few feet apart at a speed of about one mile per hour. This speed is MOST nearly equal to
    A. 1.5 feet per second
    B. 2.5 feet per second
    C. 15 feet per minute
    D. 25 feet per minute

16. Air brakes which have been applied would "creep off" most quickly by a slow leak in a
    A. main reservoir
    B. coupler hose
    C. brake pipe
    D. brake cylinder

17. By means of the equalizing piston, the pressure in the brake pipe is made equal to that in the
    A. brake cylinder
    B. equalizing reservoir
    C. main reservoir
    D. control reservoir

18. If a train operator finds it necessary to pull the emergency alarm because of heavy smoke beneath the train, the next move the train operator is required by the rules to make is to notify the
    A. nearest fire station
    B. transit police department
    C. rail control center
    D. car maintenance department

19. After coasting for some distance, a train operator on a regular subway run moves the controller handle to multiple and finds that the train does not pick up speed. In order to find out if the third rail is dead, the train operator should
    A. turn on the heater switch and check the heaters
    B. open the cab door and observe the car lights
    C. see if the tunnel lights are dark
    D. try to blow the train whistle

20. Printed instructions frequently require the train operator to secure the train. This means MOST nearly that the train operator should
    A. go to the yard and bring his train to the terminal
    B. apply the hand brakes on enough cars to hold the train
    C. get his assigned car numbers from the dispatcher
    D. cut out the fan, compressor, synchronizing and battery switches on all the cars

21. Sometimes conductors in passenger service close train doors without observing passengers entering or leaving the train. This is an improper action, chiefly because
    A. the conductor might strike a passenger with a closing door
    B. an exiting passenger might be left on the train
    C. a passenger might be left on the platform
    D. passengers who hold doors open cannot be seen

22. Before a train is to be moved from a terminal, a train operator will move the controller handle to the first point, move train about 5 feet, then shut power off. If the train moves freely, the train operator may then proceed. The MOST damaging result of operating the train if it does not roll freely in this test is
    A. slow speed
    B. overheated motors
    C. flat wheels
    D. worn brakes

23. The positions of the ME-23 brake valve handle in their respective order, from left to right, are Release, _____, Service, Emergency.
    A. Lap, Handle Off, Electric Holding
    B. Handle Off, Electric Holding, Lap
    C. Electric Holding, Handle Off, Lap
    D. Handle Off, Lap, Electric Holding

24. Compared with the older cars, the latest cars purchased by the N.Y.C.T.A. have the added feature of
    A. a slack adjuster
    B. a variable load valve
    C. automatic coupling
    D. dynamic braking

25. The normal position of the ME-23 brake valve, while the train is running between stations, is
    A. service
    B. release
    C. electric holding
    D. lap

26. If the black hand of the duplex gauge indicates 45 pounds when the controller handle of a train standing in a station is moved to an "ON" position, the train will
    A. accelerate normally
    B. accelerate very slowly
    C. remain stationary
    D. roll without power

27. Running lamps and tail lamps on trains in elevated service must be illuminated
    A. whenever the train is carrying passengers
    B. between sunrise and sunset
    C. between sunset and sunrise
    D. when the trains are operating on close headway

28. If the train operator's indication light goes dark on a regular passenger train in motion between stations, the train operator should
    A. stop the train immediately and investigate
    B. continue to the next station and then investigate
    C. whistle for a car inspector and have him investigate
    D. continue to the next station and then have the conductor buzz when doors are closed

29. The air compressor normally operates whenever the
    A. brakes are applied
    B. air pressure in the main reservoir rises above the governor setting
    C. air pressure in the main reservoir falls below the governor setting
    D. brakes are released

30. Timetables are often made up so that both local and express trains are scheduled to arrive at a station at the same time to give passengers a chance to change trains. From the passengers' viewpoint, it is MOST important for timetables to be made up in this way when the
    A. local and express trains are bound for the same terminal
    B. headways are short
    C. local and express trains are bound for different terminals
    D. headways are long

31. Since timetables showing the leaving times of all trains between 10:00 P.M. and 6:00 A.M. have been issued at subway stations, it is imperative that during these hours
    A. train operators run safely but a little faster than normally
    B. train operators run a little slower than normally
    C. conductors close the doors as soon as possible to avoid delays
    D. conductors hold the doors open at each station until the time scheduled to leave

32. All train operators are instructed that when operating trains in yards they are to operate from a standing position in the cab. The reason for this instruction is that from this position it is easier to
    A. see anyone near or approaching the track
    B. see a greater distance down the track
    C. hold down the dead man feature on the controller
    D. remain alert than it is in a sitting position

33. According to a recent bulletin, it is permissible for conductors to remove their uniform coats while on duty during a specified part of the year. It is logical to assume that the part of the year specified is from
    A. February 1st to May 15th
    B. May 15th to October 1st
    C. October 1st to December 15th
    D. December 15th to February 1st

34. A train operator would LEAST likely find yellow lanterns displayed in the subway indicating employees working on the tracks on weekdays between the hours of
    A. 7:30 A.M. and 9:30 A.M.
    B. 7:30 P.M. and 9:30 P.M.
    C. 1:30 A.M. and 3:30 A.M.
    D. 1:30 P.M. and 3:30 P.M.

35. If train operators receive a poorly executed hand or lantern signal so that they are not positive of the meaning, the BEST action for them to follow would be to
    A. proceed cautiously
    B. stop immediately
    C. disregard the signal entirely
    D. assume the most likely meaning

36. A subway train may be slow due to
    A. high third rail voltage
    B. high battery voltage
    C. a closed double cut-out cock
    D. a leaky brake pipe

37. Power from the storage batteries is used to operate the
    A. train whistle
    B. main car lights
    C. emergency lights
    D. car heaters

38. Subway car batteries are kept charged by automatically connecting the batteries in series with the
    A. main traction motors
    B. air compressor motors
    C. heaters or fan motors
    D. governor

39. The MAIN purpose of the slack adjuster is to compensate for
    A. variations in feed valve settings
    B. wearing down of brake shoes
    C. variations in passenger load
    D. wear in the brake rigging

40. A train operator operating a train with ME-23 brake valves who wants to make a 15-pound brake pipe reduction should hold the brake valve in
    A. release
    B. electric holding
    C. service
    D. emergency

40.____

KEY (CORRECT ANSWERS)

1.	C	11.	C	21.	A	31.	D
2.	D	12.	A	22.	C	32.	A
3.	C	13.	B	23.	C	33.	B
4.	B	14.	B	24.	D	34.	A
5.	D	15.	A	25.	B	35.	B
6.	A	16.	D	26.	C	36.	D
7.	D	17.	B	27.	C	37.	C
8.	D	18.	C	28.	A	38.	B
9.	C	19.	B	29.	C	39.	B
10.	B	20.	B	30.	D	40.	C

TEST 2

DIRECTIONS: Each question or incomplete statement is followed by several suggested answers or completions. Select the one that BEST answers the question or completes the statement. *PRINT THE LETTER OF THE CORRECT ANSWER IN THE SPACE AT THE RIGHT.*

1. If power goes off the third rail while a train in regular passenger service is moving between stations, the train operator should
   A. stop at the nearest blue light
   B. stop his train immediately
   C. coast as far as possible
   D. coast to the next station if possible

   1.____

2. The purpose of the main reservoir safety valve is to
   A. maintain constant air pressure in the main reservoir
   B. protect the main reservoir against excessive air pressure
   C. cut out the compressor motor if it runs too long
   D. indicate when the pressure in the main reservoir is too low to operate the air brakes

   2.____

3. The force that pushes the brake cylinder piston back when the brakes are released is supplied by
   A. a spring   B. an electric motor
   C. compressed air   D. a counter-weight

   3.____

4. A passenger claiming to have lost an umbrella should be directed to apply to the Lost and Found Office at
   A. 34th Street/8th Avenue Mezzanine   B. 3961 10th Avenue
   C. 73 Rockwell Place   D. 2545 7th Avenue

   4.____

5. Some cars used by the N.Y.C.T.A. are equipped with dynamic brakes. Such brakes help bring a train to a stop by causing the
   A. contact shoes to be lifted from the third rail
   B. air brakes to exert a positive force on the brake shoes
   C. driving motors to act as a braking force
   D. dynamic brakes to clasp on separate brake drums

   5.____

6. The MOST effective and practical way for train operators to bring a moving subway train to an emergency stop is for them to
   A. open the conductor's emergency valve
   B. remove his hand from the brake valve handle
   C. reverse the reverser keeping power on
   D. remove their hand from the master controller handle

   6.____

7. Employees of the transit system must always take the safe course in the performance of their duties. In order to follow the "safe course," a train operator should
   A. not try to make up lost time
   B. watch all stop arms to see that they are not clamped down
   C. refuse to accept a direction to proceed from a signal maintainer in the face of a red over red signal
   D. never center the reverser with the train in motion

8. The crew of a train which is stalled should make every effort to obtain information about the cause of the delay and should announce to passengers the cause and probable duration. The MOST important reason for making such announcement is to
   A. keep the crew occupied
   B. show that transit employees know their job
   C. avoid confusion and apprehension among passengers
   D. help clear up the trouble

9. If a train crew requires technical assistance to move a disabled train in passenger service, the employees who could help the crew most would be
   A. dispatcher and tower operator
   B. road car inspector and train service supervisor
   C. train operator instructor and signal maintainer
   D. road car inspector and superintendent

10. Loss of third rail power on a subway car will first prevent functioning of the
    A. car emergency lights
    B. service brakes
    C. pneumatically operated doors
    D. air compressor

11. When it is necessary for train operators to descend to the track while looking for brake trouble on a stalled passenger train, an approved safety precaution would be to
    A. take the reverser key and brake handle with them
    B. have a conductor place a red lantern at least 50 feet to the rear of the train
    C. chock the front and rear wheels of one car
    D. station a conductor on the rear end of the train

12. When a train operator has slippered a contact shoe, it means that he has
    A. applied grease to the underside of the contact shoe
    B. stopped the train so that a contact shoe is in a third rail gap
    C. placed a shoe paddle between the third rail and the contact shoe
    D. removed an old type contact shoe and replaced it with a new type

13. After making a regular station stop, a subway train operator finds that they cannot start their train and that the emergency car lights are on. In this case it would be logical to assume that
    A. someone had pulled the emergency alarm box
    B. someone had pulled the conductor's emergency cord
    C. the train had split in two
    D. the subway section was flooded to a depth of at least one foot

14. When a train operator's indication light is illuminated, it is an indication that
    A. the third rail is alive   B. all brakes are released
    C. all side doors are closed   D. the batteries are fully charged

15. The switching position of the master controller should not be used as a running position for a prolonged period principally because
    A. automatic trips are not installed on most yard tracks
    B. the train would move too slowly
    C. it is difficult to make a smooth stop from switching speed
    D. the starting resistors may burn out

16. One purpose of the electric feature of the electro-pneumatic brake is to
    A. hold the original brake application until the train stops
    B. apply the brakes equally on all cars at the same time
    C. ensure a smooth final stop
    D. start all compressors at the same time

17. The BEST way for a train operator to acquaint himself with new regulations as soon as possible is to
    A. read all the new bulletins when he signs in
    B. study the book of rules
    C. be alert to the needs of the service
    D. depend on the dispatcher to keep him up to date

18. A train collided with a door of an inspection shop. This accident was MOST likely caused by
    A. the train operator's failure to blow the whistle before the entrance as required by the rules
    B. the train operator's failure to stop 50 feet before the entrance as required by the rules
    C. high third rail voltage
    D. defective service or emergency brakes

19. Of the following actions of a train operator, the one which would NOT be considered a violation of the rules would be to
    A. coast between stations with the reverser centered
    B. operate in regular passenger service with the cab door open
    C. stop the train in a station a car length beyond the car stop marker
    D. sound several blasts of the whistle when skipping a regular passenger station

20. A moving train is normally brought to a stop by manipulating the brake valve handle so as to cause compressed air to be
    A. exhausted from the brake cylinder
    B. exhausted from the brake pipe
    C. admitted to the brake pipe
    D. admitted to the main reservoir

20.____

21. If a conductor finds it necessary to cut out a door enroute, the conductor should
    A. first telephone the superintendent for permission to do so
    B. do so and notify a car inspector at the first opportunity
    C. telephone the dispatcher to repair door when the train arrives at the terminal
    D. notify the train operator instructor at the first opportunity but continue on to the terminal

21.____

22. When a train is enroute and a car inspector and police officer is required, the conductor shall pass the prescribed buzzer signal to the train operator
    A. if he has first checked with the other conductor that assistance is really needed
    B. after the train has stopped at the station where assistance can be obtained
    C. after he has first opened the nearest conductor's valve
    D. as the train is approaching the station where assistance can be obtained

22.____

23. If one contact shoe of a car is touching the third rail, a train operator should know that the number of shoes alive on that car is
    A. 4   B. 3   C. 2   D. 1

23.____

24. A train operator on the subway system knows that door engine magnet valves are located
    A. in the train operator's cab
    B. under the car body
    C. under car seats
    D. at the conductor's door operating controls

24.____

25. Opening the trip cock on a subway car will ordinarily result in
    A. releasing the brakes
    B. a service brake application
    C. an emergency brake application
    D. uncoupling the cars

25.____

26. When the three amber lights located above the platform for a particular track at a gap station are lighted, it means that the
    A. conductor should close doors immediately
    B. train operator should notify the conductor by whistle to close doors if he does not get an indication
    C. dispatcher is ordering train out of the station as soon as possible
    D. conductor must keep doors of the train open

26.____

27. The rules state that a train operator traveling through an under-river tunnel is limited to a maximum speed of _____ MPH.
    A. 15 B. 25 C. 35 D. 40

28. Three yellow lanterns hanging one above another to the right of a track means
    A. a flagman ahead; watch for his signal
    B. a temporary speed restriction of 10 miles per hour
    C. stop, and then proceed according to rules
    D. look for two yellow lanterns to be displayed, further on, a distance of 300 feet from this point

29. The train operator's whistle signal for a car inspector is _____ blasts.
    A. two long
    B. three short
    C. three long
    D. a succession of short

30. A train operator is NOT required to stop his train when he sees a
    A. green lantern placed between the rails
    B. red lantern waved up and down
    C. yellow lantern waved back and forth across the track
    D. white lantern near platform edge at entering end of the station

KEY (CORRECT ANSWERS)

1. D	11. A	21. B
2. B	12. C	22. D
3. A	13. A	23. A
4. A	14. C	24. C
5. C	15. D	25. C
6. D	16. B	26. D
7. D	17. A	27. C
8. C	18. B	28. B
9. B	19. D	29. B
10. D	20. B	30. D

EXAMINATION SECTION
TEST 1

DIRECTIONS: Each question or incomplete statement is followed by several suggested answers or completions. Select the one that BEST answers the question or completes the statement. *PRINT THE LETTER OF THE CORRECT ANSWER IN THE SPACE AT THE RIGHT.*

1. The LEAST important reason for a train operator to keep his train exactly on schedule time in rush hours is that a train which is
   A. ahead of schedule has to be held at time points
   B. behind schedule is likely to cause delays at junctions
   C. ahead of schedule does not carry its share of the load
   D. behind schedule is likely to become overcrowded and further delayed

   1.____

2. Three principal fixed signal indications are PROCEED, PROCEED WITH CAUTION, AND STOP. The PROCEED indication means MOST nearly
   A. go as fast as the train can go
   B. go at normal speed for the particular track condition
   C. no need to slow down before reaching the next signal
   D. go at not over 35 miles per hour

   2.____

3. The law requires that subway cars in passenger service during the winter season must be kept heated to between 40 and 64 degrees. It is MOST likely that these particular limits were picked because they
   A. are most economical
   B. result in minimum year-round temperatures
   C. are the most comfortable year-round temperatures
   D. are comfortable for passengers wearing outdoor clothing

   3.____

4. The term "automatic stop" as used on the transit system means a
   A. train stop which is not initiated by the train operator
   B. device on the roadway which applies the brakes when a train passes a red signal
   C. device used on cars to apply the brakes in an emergency
   D. scheduled stop for an express operating on the local track

   4.____

5. One function of the emergency alarm system in the subway is to
   A. sound a warning in the nearest firehouse
   B. supply power to the car emergency lights
   C. provide a means of communication in the event of a power failure
   D. remove power from the third rail

   5.____

6. When the train operator of a passenger train descends to the track to check the train because the brakes fail to release, the train operator need NOT
   A. set up a hand brake
   B. take the reverser key
   C. pull the emergency alarm
   D. inform the conductor

   6.____

7. Trains are operated in both directions on a single track in under-river tunnels whenever certain kinds of work must be done, alternate trains running in opposite directions. If the running time between the two towers at the ends of a certain tunnel is 3½ minutes, the MINIMUM headway in one direction when such single-tracking is operated is _____ minutes.
   A. 14   B. 10½   C. 7   D. 3½

Questions 8-15.

DIRECTIONS: Questions 8 through 15 inclusive in Column I are descriptions of lantern signals, each of which has one of the meanings listed in Column II. For each item in Column I, select the associated meaning from Column II.

Column I

Column II

8. A single yellow lantern suspended on the right-hand side of the track

9. One green lantern suspended on the right-hand side of the track

10. Three yellow lanterns arranged vertically on the right-hand side of the track

11. A single yellow lantern standing on the track between the rails

12. Two yellow lanterns suspended one above the other on the right-hand side of the track

13. A yellow lantern waved up and down by a flagman

14. One red lantern on the right-hand side of the track

15. A white light waved back and forth across the track

A. Bring train under control and blow warning for employees working on the track
B. Stop
C. Resume normal operation in accordance with fixed signals
D. Reduce train speed to 10 MPH and hold it until the end of the temporary slow speed section is reached
E. Proceed cautiously to the next flagman

16. When third rail power fails, one effect on a train is that the
    A. emergency car lights will not light
    B. brakes cannot be applied in an emergency
    C. doors cannot be opened
    D. air compressors will not start

17. If the hand brake wheel or lever cannot be moved easily to release the brake, the release can be made easy by
    A. applying power to the motors for an instant
    B. placing the nearest brake valve in release
    C. making an emergency brake application
    D. closing the double cut-out cock for a few seconds

    17.____

18. A train operator should be particularly alert to guard against sliding the wheels on a yard track
    A. at the beginning of a light rain
    B. immediately after the rails have been polished
    C. when the rails have been renewed
    D. during a long dry spell

    18.____

19. A train operator operating a train on a yard layup track toward a single car standing ahead notices a red lantern displayed on the rear of the car. Particular caution should be exercised in approaching this car because the red lantern indicates that
    A. the car is against the bumping block
    B. employees may be at work beneath the car
    C. air brake is inoperative and no hand brake is set up
    D. the car is close to the main line

    19.____

20. The protection of the "dead-man" feature on a moving train is lost when the
    A. reverser is centered   B. brakes are applied in emergency
    C. train is coasting   D. electric brake is not cut in

    20.____

21. The red hand of the duplex air gauge indicates the pressure in the
    A. main reservoir   B. brake cylinder
    C. equalizing reservoir   D. control reservoir

    21.____

22. The black hand of the duplex air gauge indicates the pressure in the
    A. main reservoir   B. brake cylinder
    C. equalizing reservoir   D. control reservoir

    22.____

23. The one of the following which could NOT be the cause for a train running slow is
    A. weak batteries   B. high third rail voltage
    C. brake pipe leak   D. hand brake not fully released

    23.____

24. If the main reservoir hand in the leading cab of a ten-car train falls rapidly when the brake handle is returned to release after a 20 lb. pneumatic reduction has been made, it indicates that the
    A. main reservoirs were not fully charged
    B. main reservoir line is not continuous for the full length of the train
    C. brakes are performing satisfactorily
    D. brake valve in another car is in release

    24.____

25. The MOST likely result of a short main reservoir line is that
    A. brakes may be slow in releasing
    B. compressors may fail due to being overloaded
    C. protection of the dead-man feature may be lost
    D. normal brake valve manipulation may cause an emergency application

26. The puff of air heard after cutting in the electric braked and making the test described is a positive indication that the
    A. brakes may be applied electrically throughout the train
    B. electric brake fuse at the operating position is blown
    C. brakes may be released electrically from any cab
    D. release magnet on the head car was energized

27. The full reduction made electrically guards against moving the train with a closed _____ of the train.
    A. brake pipe angle cock at either end
    B. main reservoir pipe angle cock at either end
    C. main reservoir pipe angle cock in the middle
    D. brake pipe angle cock in the middle

28. If the train does not roll freely when the controller is moved to the first point and then shut off, the BEST course for the train operator is to
    A. stop and have the conductor help him check to see that all hand brakes are off
    B. notch up the controller and try again at a higher speed
    C. stop, apply the hand brake, and call the superintendent
    D. make a running test of the brakes

29. After cars have been added to a train at a terminal, the brakes must be applied in emergency from the cars which have been added. The purpose of making the brake application from the added cars is to check that
    A. angle cocks are open throughout the train
    B. air compressors on the added cars are working
    C. there is no air leakage at the coupler
    D. brake valves in both sections are functioning

30. If it is necessary in an emergency to reverse the motors of a moving train when the controller is in an ON position, the train operator should
    A. release the controller handle, reverse the reverser, then depress the controller handle
    B. release the controller handle, move it to OFF, reverse the reverser, then depress the controller handle and move it to an ON position
    C. place the brake handle in emergency and move the controller to OFF, reverse the reverser, then move the controller handle to an ON position
    D. reverse the reverser, move the controller to OFF and place the brake handle in emergency, then move the controller to an ON position

31. A train operator finds a male passenger asleep on a train just laid up in a yard. The BEST action for the train operator to take is to
    A. escort the passenger to the nearest yard gate and let him out
    B. take the passenger to crew quarters so that he can leave with the next man clearing
    C. move the passenger to the end car, cut it off, and run it back to the terminal
    D. call the dispatcher via radio and tell them there is a customer on the train

32. Upon approaching a dark dwarf signal with a lay-up train in a yard, the BEST action for the train operator to take is to stop and then
    A. proceed with caution if the switch is properly lined up
    B. blow the proper train whistle signal to attack the tower operator/dispatcher's attention
    C. wait for a shop employee to flag him by the signal
    D. change ends and go back to the dispatcher's office

33. Road train operator's reporting time at terminals are commonly ten minutes before their trains are scheduled to depart. One reason for having this time interval is to allow the train operator to
    A. check that his conductor has signed in
    B. read the latest bulletin orders
    C. make reports of unusual occurrences
    D. bring the train in from the yard

34. The scheduled round trip time on a certain line, including layover time for the train crew at both terminals, is one hour. The MINIMUM number of train crews required to maintain a ten minute headway on this line between midnight and 4 A.M. is
    A. 6   B. 12   C. 18   D. 24

35. When a train operator approaches an interlocking where they are scheduled to take a diverging route, the signal displayed should be
    A. green over red   B. green over green
    C. green or yellow over yellow D. green or yellow over green

KEY (CORRECT ANSWERS)

1.	A	11.	B	21.	A	31.	D
2.	B	12.	A	22.	C	32.	B
3.	D	13.	E	23.	B	33.	B
4.	B	14.	B	24.	B	34.	A
5.	D	15.	B	25.	A	35.	C
6.	C	16.	D	26.	D		
7.	C	17.	C	27.	D		
8.	A	18.	A	28.	A		
9.	C	19.	B	29.	A		
10.	D	20.	A	30.	C		

TEST 2

DIRECTIONS: Each question or incomplete statement is followed by several suggested answers or completions. Select the one that BEST answers the question or completes the statement. *PRINT THE LETTER OF THE CORRECT ANSWER IN THE SPACE AT THE RIGHT.*

1. The double cut-out cock on the fifth car of an eight-car train is closed. If the train operator makes a brake application from the leading cab, the brakes will be applied on   1.____
    A. the first four cars only
    B. the fifth car only
    C. all but the fifth car
    D. all but the last three cars

2. If you do not feel sure that you understand a bulletin covering signal changes at a certain point on your route, you should   2.____
    A. call the superintendent
    B. ask the signal maintainer to explain it
    C. plan to be especially cautious when proceeding through that section
    D. discuss it with the dispatcher

3. Call-on signals are displayed on _____ signals.   3.____
    A. home   B. dwarf   C. approach   D. automatic

4. The purpose of a contact shoe slipper is to   4.____
    A. insulate the contact shoe from the third rail
    B. make the shoe slide easily on the third rail
    C. keep the third rail clean during a snowstorm
    D. provide a place to mount the shoe on the truck

5. If a train which has just been coupled parts when taking a "stretch," the yard train operator should   5.____
    A. apply hand brakes on both sections and call the dispatcher for orders
    B. blow for a car inspector
    C. get into the other section and couple from there
    D. recouple at normal speed and take another "stretch"

6. The rules state that train operators moving trains into the inspection shed must "pull into the shed slowly, taking into consideration the condition of the shop tracks, brakes, and the length of their train. The LEAST probable reason for such caution is that   6.____
    A. tracks in inspection sheds may be slippery
    B. shop employees may be working on or near the track
    C. long inspection trains must be pulled further into the shed than short ones
    D. bumping blocks in inspection sheds are of lightweight construction

2 (#2)

7. Train operators are sometimes required to read and sign individual copies of a special order, and the signed copies are then filed in the train operator's records. This procedure is MOST likely to be used when
   A. a rule which has been widely violated is to be rigidly enforced
   B. single tack is to be operated in an under-river tunnel for several nights in succession
   C. express trains are to run local at night because of track reconstruction
   D. new car equipment is placed in operation for the first time

7.____

8. Hand brakes are to be set up on two cars of an eight-car train laid up on a grade. If the cars are numbered from 1 to 8 starting with the car that is highest on the grade, it would be BEST to set up the hand brakes on cars
   A. 1 and 2   B. 2 and 7   C. 3 and 6   D. 7 and 8

8.____

9. A train operator has not timed his brake application correctly and can see that the train will stop with several cars beyond the station if he continues to brake normally. His BEST action is to sound the appropriate signal to warn the conductor and then
   A. sound the signal to warn people on the platform
   B. make a smooth stop
   C. skip the station
   D. apply the brakes in emergency

9.____

10. When the brakes are fully released, the black hand of the duplex gauge should indicate about _____ lbs.
    A. 50   B. 60   C. 70   D. 90

10.____

11. After applying the required number of hand brakes on a train which has been laid up on a steep grade, the PROPER test of whether the hand brakes will hold the train is to
    A. apply the brakes in emergency
    B. examine each hand brake chain to see that it is tight
    C. place the brake valve in release
    D. open the compressor switches

11.____

12. The rules state that "train operators must approach all STOP signals, trains ahead, junctions, and terminals with train under full control." Having the train "under full control" means MOST NEARLY
    A. operating your train so that you can stop it smoothly within your range of vision
    B. having your reverser forward, master controller off, and brake handle in release
    C. standing with both your hands on the controls, prepared to make an emergency stop
    D. slowing your train down to 10 MPH and holding that speed

12.____

13. Before starting out of a terminal, the train operator must   13.____
    A. receive a proceed buzzer signal from the conductor
    B. check that the starting lights are on
    C. have a green leaving signal
    D. sound the appropriate whistle signal

14. Approaching the low point of a straight section of track on a four-track   14.____
    subway line, the train operator of an express train observes that water is
    coming in through a ventilator and has covered the roadbed so the top of the
    running rails for a distance about equal to the length of his train. If the
    automatic signal in the center of the flooded section is green, the train operator
    should
    A. place the controller in multiple to get through the flooded section quickly
    B. proceed slowly through the flooded section and report it at the next
       station
    C. stop and blow the train whistle for assistance
    D. stop and telephone for orders

15. By logical reasoning, it should be clear that the two most used positions of   15.____
    the master controller on trains in regular passenger service are
    A. off and switching   B. switching and series
    C. series and multiple   D. multiple and off

16. The train operator of a local train coasting down the grade between two   16.____
    stations becomes aware of a grounded shoe beam by the severe arcing and
    acrid fumes coming from the shoe beneath the cab. The WISEST course is to
    A. stop immediately and open the main switch
    B. continue to the next station before taking any other action
    C. stop at the nearest emergency exit and discharge passengers
    D. whistle for a car inspector

17. At about 8:00 A.M. on a weekday, the train operator of a local train which is   17.____
    standing at a station sees a broken rail on the adjacent express track. The
    BEST immediate action is to apply the brakes in emergency and then
    A. blow the whistle until the express stops
    B. notify the rail control center via radio
    C. notify a station employee to call the superintendent
    D. call the preceding time point to hold the express

18. The MOST likely cause of a dark train operator's indication is   18.____
    A. bulb burned out   B. reverser off center
    C. side door open   D. battery fuse blown

19. The New York City Transit Authority currently has how many different levels   19.____
    in the Cold Weather Plan?
    A. Four
    B. Five
    C. Six
    D. Varies depending on the strength of the storm

20. What is NOT considered part of a train operator's operational equipment? 20.____
   A. Safety vest
   B. Brake handle
   C. Employee badge
   D. Rulebook

KEY (CORRECT ANSWERS)

1.	C	11.	C
2.	D	12.	A
3.	A	13.	A
4.	A	14.	B
5.	D	15.	D
6.	D	16.	B
7.	A	17.	B
8.	D	18.	C
9.	B	19.	C
10.	C	20.	C

EXAMINATION SECTION

TEST 1

DIRECTIONS: Each question or incomplete statement is followed by several suggested answers or completions. Select the one that BEST answers the question or completes the statement. *PRINT THE LETTER OF THE CORRECT ANSWER IN THE SPACE AT THE RIGHT.*

1. There is NO rapid transit tunnel of the N.Y.C.T.A. under the East River at _____ Street.
   A. 34th   B. 42nd   C. 53rd   D. 60th

   1._____

2. A train is laid up in a repair yard because it has lost its compressed air. It would still be both possible and permissible to
   A. apply the air brakes
   B. operate the train
   C. release the air brakes
   D. operate the fans

   2._____

3. When the air brakes are released, the force which keeps them released is supplied by
   A. compressed air
   B. counter weights
   C. magnetism
   D. coil springs

   3._____

4. While a train is braking to a regular stop at a passenger station, third rail power fails. The train operator would surely become aware of this failure when
   A. the brakes applied in emergency automatically
   B. he tried to start after the station stop
   C. the train stopped short of the car stop marker
   D. the train stopped beyond the car stop marker

   4._____

5. According to recent instructions, extra care shall be exercised in operating trains approaching bumper blocks, bar doors, and terminals. The reason for this extra care is that at these locations
   A. moves are generally protected by block signals
   B. workers might be on or near the tracks
   C. trains are more likely to skid
   D. more expensive equipment could be damaged

   5._____

6. The MOST serious result of improperly displayed marker lights at the front end of a train could be to
   A. increase the time interval between trains
   B. confuse those passengers who know train destinations by the color of the marker
   C. cause a platform man to announce wrong information
   D. confuse trackwalkers

   6._____

7. Certain work motors have four trip cocks and a special device which controls the air to the trip cocks so that these cars can be operated safely on any division. This special device is a _____ valve.
   A. brake   B. transfer   C. diversion   D. pilot

8. The electric portion slide is a part of the
   A. coupler
   B. brake valve
   C. door engine
   D. master controller

9. An INCORRECT statement to make about N.Y.C.T.A. subway cars that are NOT *married pairs* is that some of them have exactly
   A. two motors
   B. four motors
   C. two uncoupling valves
   D. four uncoupling valves

10. The practice of *taking a stretch* when making up trains is to test the
    A. brakes   B. couplers   C. motors   D. side doors

11. When an emergency alarm box in the subway is pulled, power will be removed from the third raid and, in addition,
    A. an alarm will be sounded in the nearest firehouse
    B. the local telephone will be connected directly to the rail control center
    C. an alarm will be sounded in the rail control center
    D. the brakes on all trains in the area will apply in emergency

12. The crew of a disabled train in regular passenger service has not been able to find out why the train will not move. The titles of the employees who could help the crew MOST in this situation would be
    A. road car inspector and superintendent
    B. train operator instructor and signal maintainer
    C. dispatcher and tower operator
    D. road car inspector and train operator instructor

13. One result of a train operator running ahead of schedule is to
    A. overload his follower
    B. overload his leader
    C. delay his own train
    D. delay his leader

14. The cutting key is MOST closely associated in operation with a
    A. brake valve
    B. master controller
    C. contact shoe
    D. coupler

15. If a speed of 15 miles per hour is exactly 22 feet per second, then the number of miles per hour corresponding to 40 feet per second is MOST NEARLY
    A. 10   B. 20   C. 25   D. 30

16. If the average speed of a train is 20 MPH, the time it takes the train to travel 1 mile is _____ minutes.
    A. 2   B. 3   C. 4   D. 5

3 (#1)

17. If the average speed of a train between two stations is 30 miles per hour, and the two stations are ½ mile apart, the time it takes the train to travel from one station to the other is _____ minute(s).
     A. 1   B. 2   C. 3   D. 4

18. A layup yard has five equal-length tracks that can hold a total of 55 cars. If 8 cars are laid up on one track and six cars on each of the other four, the additional number of cars that can be laid up in this yard is
     A. 8   B. 23   C. 24   D. 32

19. If twelve ten-car trains and eight eight-car trains pass a point on a certain track during one hour, the headway on that track is _____ minutes.
     A. 6   B. 5   C. 4   D. 3

20. The running time of a train between two terminals is 48 minutes, and there is a 7-minute layover at each terminal. If a train leaves one terminal at 11:00 A.M., this train is due back at the same terminal at
     A. 11:48 A.M.   B. 11:55 A.M.   C. 12:43 P.M.   D. 12:50 P.M.

21. A train operator's weekly pay for 8 hours a day, 5 days a week, at $13.32 an hour is
     A. $533.20   B. $532.80   C. $528.80   D. $493.20

22. The voltage of the storage battery on subway cars is NEAREST to _____ volts.
     A. 20   B. 35   C. 50   D. 65

23. Because of a blockade, an express train is routed to the local tracks. Unless otherwise instructed, this train should stop at
     A. express stations only
     B. all stations
     C. certain predetermined busy stations only
     D. every other station

Questions 24-36.

DIRECTIONS: Questions 24 through 36, inclusive, are based on the R-10 or later type passenger cars equipped with ME-42 brake valves.

24. According to the latest instructions, before moving a car, the brake pipe pressure and the straight air pipe pressure should be, respectively, _____ pounds.
     A. 90 and 70   B. 80 and 60   C. 70 and 90   D. 60 and 80

25. The black hand on the duplex air gage indicates the pressure in the
     A. straight air pipe   B. brake cylinder
     C. brake pipe   D. compressor

26. The speed that must be reached before the dynamic brakes become effective is AT LEAST _____ MPH
    A. 5   B. 10   C. 15   D. 20

27. The length of these cars is either _____ feet.
    A. 36 or 40   B. 41 or 50   C. 51 or 60   D. 61 or 67

28. When the brake valve handle is in its extreme right-hand position, the ME-42 brake valve is in
    A. release   B. service   C. emergency   D. handle off

29. The proper position of the ME-42 brake valve when running normally over the road is
    A. electric holding
    B. running release
    C. full release
    D. handle off

30. The couplers used on these cars are designated by the symbol
    A. J1   B. F   C. H2C   D. J1F

31. On a ten-car train set up for two-conductor operation, the number of drum switches that must be set in the OFF position is
    A. 2   B. 4   C. 6   D. 8

32. Operation of the brakes on these cars is similar to the operation of the brakes on a passenger automobile MAINLY in that
    A. hydraulic brakes are used on both trains and cars
    B. air brakes are used on both trains and cars
    C. there is an individual brake cylinder for each wheel
    D. the greater the motion of the brake handle or pedal, the greater the braking effect

33. The number of brake cylinders on these cars is
    A. 1   B. 2   C. 4   D. 8

34. The function of the door relay on these cars is to
    A. close the control circuit after all doors are closed
    B. stop the train if a door opens while the train is moving
    C. permit operation of all doors in the train from one point
    D. prevent opening the door while the train is in motion

35. The brakes on these cars will NOT apply in emergency if the master controller handle is released when the reverse handle is forward and the brake valve is in
    A. full release
    B. full service
    C. running release
    D. handle-off

5 (#1)

36. To cut out the brakes on a car, the train operator should
    A. pull up the brake cylinder cut-out cock
    B. put the brake valve in release
    C. open the synchronizing line wire
    D. open one of the trip cocks

36._____

37. A train being brought to a stop from a speed of 30 MPH would be LEAST likely to skid if the track is
    A. slightly rusted and dry
    B. slightly rusted and wet
    C. well polished and wet
    D. well polished and dry

37._____

38. After being signaled to slow down by lanterns because employees are working on the tracks, a train operator should expect to see a signal beyond the track work indicating that he can resume speed. In MOST cases, this signal should be placed beyond the work a distance of about _____ feet.
    A. 75   B. 150   C. 300   D. 600

38._____

39. Referring to Question 38 above, the color of the signal which indicates to the train operator that he should slow down is
    A. red   B. white   C. blue   D. yellow

39._____

40. Route request buttons are installed on certain signals where there is a choice of route. If the signal indicates the wrong route or stop, the train operator can request the correct route by stopping at the signal and
    A. blowing four short whistle blasts
    B. telephoning the signal tower
    C. pressing the button corresponding to the desired route
    D. pressing the button a number of times to correspond with the number of the route requested

40._____

41. A lighted operator's indication informs the operator that
    A. brake pipe pressure has fallen below normal
    B. all side doors are closed and locked
    C. no hand brakes are applied
    D. the train battery is charged

41._____

42. According to rules, when an operator is about to operate his train into an inspection shed, he must blow two distinct blasts on his whistle, then pull into the shed slowly. The MOST likely reason for blowing the whistle is to
    A. summon a shop employee to attach a power lead
    B. notify the tower operator to clear the entering signal
    C. notify the conductor that he is going into the shed
    D. warn shop employees of the approach of his train

42._____

Questions 43-48.

DIRECTIONS: Questions 43 through 48, inclusive, in Column I are operating situations where the speed of trains is restricted by N.Y.C.T.A. rules to one of the maximum speeds listed in Column II. For each operating situation given in Column I, select the MAXIMUM allowable speed from Column II.

Column I	Column II	
43. Running on clear signals in under-river tubes	A. 10 MPH B. 15 MPH C. Series speed D. 35 MPH	43.____
44. Moving over diverging routes unless otherwise indicated		44.____
45. Entering terminals unless otherwise indicated		45.____
46. Running on straight track in a yard		46.____
47. Passing a station without stopping		47.____
48. Operating over switches in a yard		48.____

49. A train operator brought his passenger train to a stop and waited for a few second at an automatic signal indicating stop, then pulled past the insulated joint and watched the automatic stop arm clear. He then proceeded slowly to the next signal. This train operator
    A. operated his train correctly according to the rules
    B. should have stayed at the signal much longer
    C. should not have passed a signal indicating stop
    D. should have whistled for the signal maintainer before proceeding

49.____

50. The train operator's whistle signal to call a police officer is
    A. long-short-long-short   B. short-long-short-long
    C. short-short-short   D. long-long-long

50.____

KEY (CORRECT ANSWERS)

1.	A	11.	C	21.	B	31.	B	41.	B
2.	D	12.	D	22.	B	32.	D	42.	D
3.	D	13.	A	23.	A	33.	C	43.	D
4.	B	14.	D	24.	A	34.	A	44.	A
5.	A	15.	C	25.	C	35.	B	45.	B
6.	C	16.	B	26.	C	36.	A	46.	C
7.	C	17.	A	27.	C	37.	D	47.	B
8.	A	18.	B	28.	D	38.	D	48.	A
9.	C	19.	D	29.	B	39.	D	49.	A
10.	B	20.	C	30.	C	40.	C	50.	A

TEST 2

DIRECTIONS: Each question or incomplete statement is followed by several suggested answers or completions. Select the one that BEST answers the question or completes the statement. *PRINT THE LETTER OF THE CORRECT ANSWER IN THE SPACE AT THE RIGHT.*

1. The train operator's whistle signal to call a car inspector is
   A. long-short-long-short
   B. short-long-short-long
   C. short-short-short
   D. long-long-long

2. A train must NOT be operated for long periods with its master controller held in the switching position because such operation could cause the
   A. accelerating resistance to burn out
   B. train to accelerate too slowly
   C. train to accelerate too rapidly
   D. storage batteries to discharge excessively

3. If power should go off the third rail while a train is in motion between stations, the train operator should
   A. coast to the nearest station, emergency exit, or emergency telephone location if possible
   B. coast to the nearest home signal or automatic signal location if possible
   C. coast as far as possible
   D. make an emergency stop immediately

Questions 4-8.

DIRECTIONS: Questions 4 through 8, inclusive, refer to the paragraph PROCEDURE FOR FLAGGING DISABLED TRAIN given below. Consult the paragraph when answering these questions.

PROCEDURE FOR FLAGGING DISABLED TRAIN

If at any time it becomes necessary to operate a train from other than the forward cab of the leading car, a qualified Rapid Transit Transportation Department employee must be stationed on the forward end. The train operator and the aforesaid qualified employee must have a clear understanding as to the signals to be used between them as well as to the method of operation. They must know, by actual test, that they have communication between them. Flagging signals should be given at short intervals while train is in motion. If the train is carrying passengers, they must be discharged at the next station. Train operators operating from other than the forward cab of the leading car must not advance the controlled beyond the series position.

4. The qualified employee stationed at the forward end must NOT be a
   A. train operator
   B. conductor
   C. train operator instructor
   D. road car inspector

5. While the train is in motion, the employees stationed at the forward end should give a flagging signal
   A. at frequent intervals
   B. every time the train is about to pass a fixed signal
   C. only when he wants the train speed changed
   D. only when he wants to check his understanding with the train operator

6. Train operators operating from other than the leading car must NOT advance the controller beyond
   A. switching   B. series   C. multiple   D. parallel

7. Considering the actual conditions on a passenger train in the subway, the MOST practical method of communication between the operator and the employee at the forward end would be by using the
   A. train public address system   B. buzzer signals
   C. whistle signals   D. lantern signals

8. The BEST reason for discharging passengers at the next station under these conditions is that
   A. carrying passengers would cause additional delays
   B. it is not possible to operate safely
   C. the train operator cannot see the station stop markers
   D. the four lights at the front of the train will be red

9. A train operator is walking on the tracks near a switch. From a safety standpoint, he should be LEAST concerned about
   A. the third rail   B. grease on the ties
   C. falling objects   D. switch movements

10. After giving you an order over the phone, the train dispatcher is likely to ask you to repeat the order back to him to be sure that you
    A. will carry out the order as given
    B. are capable of carrying out the order
    C. have heard the order as given
    D. have made a written record of the order

Questions 11-26.

DIRECTIONS: Questions 11 through 26, inclusive, are based on the accompanying illustrations of color-light signals, signs, and markers used on the transit system. In the illustrations, the colors are illuminated signs, W denotes a white illuminated sign, and S denotes an illuminated S sign.

11. This signal indicates
    A. stop and stay
    B. stop and then proceed, prepared to stop within vision
    C. proceed with caution at allowable speed
    D. proceed

12. This signal indicates
    A. stop and stay
    B. stop and then proceed, prepared to stop within vision
    C. proceed with caution at allowable speed
    D. proceed with caution

13. The indication of this signal is
    A. proceed with caution
    B. stop and then proceed, prepared to stop within vision
    C. proceed with caution at allowable speed
    D. proceed

14. This signal means
    A. stop and then proceed, prepared to stop within vision
    B. proceed with caution
    C. proceed with caution at allowable speed
    D. proceed expecting to find track occupied

15. The non-illuminated sign shown means
    A. cut-in power
    B. cut-out lights
    C. car stop
    D. coast

16. The indication of this illuminated sign is
    A. do not exceed indicated speed on curve
    B. beginning of time control at indicated speed
    C. take turnout at indicated speed
    D. approaching a terminal, maintain indicated speed

17. This sign means that
    A. there are no speed restrictions beyond this point
    B. signals beyond this point do not apply to trains
    C. train operators may operate without regard to rules beyond this point
    D. block signaling ends at this point

18. The non-illuminated sign shown is the
    A. station stop marker for 8-car trains
    B. turning point marker for 8-car trains
    C. beginning of coasting marker for 8-car trains
    D. marker for the point at which a 8-car train may resume normal speed

19. This sign is the
    A. station stop marker for 8-car trains
    B. turning point marker for 8-car trains
    C. beginning of coasting marker for 8-car trains
    D. marker for the point at which a 8-car train may resume normal speed

19._____

20. This signal aspect means proceed
    A. normally on either route
    B. at not exceeding 25 MPH on main route
    C. normally on diverging route
    D. normally on main route

20._____

21. This signal aspect means proceed on
    A. diverging route expecting next signal to be red
    B. main route expecting next signal to be red
    C. on diverging route expecting next signal to be clear
    D. main route expecting next signal to be clear

21._____

22. This signal aspect means that a train operator may proceed on
    A. diverging route expecting next signal to be red
    B. main route expecting next signal to be red
    C. diverging route expecting next signal to be clear
    D. main route expecting next signal to be clear

22._____

23. The indication shown is proceed
    A. on main route
    B. with caution on diverging route
    C. on diverging route
    D. with caution on main route

23.____

24. The aspect shown means
    A. stop and signal for route
    B. stop, operate stop release, then proceed with caution, prepared to stop
    C. stop and wait for a less restrictive aspect
    D. stop and telephone for orders

24.____

25. The indication shown would MOST probably permit a train operator to
    A. operate the stop release and then proceed with caution
    B. operate the hand throw switch and then proceed with caution
    C. enter inspection shed with caution
    D. proceed with caution onto yard lead

25.____

26. This illuminated sign is the
    A. station stop marker for 10-car trains
    B. turning point marker for 10-car trains
    C. beginning of coasting marker for 10-car trains
    D. marker for the point at which a 10-car train may resume normal speed

26.____

27. One item which is NOT present on both cars of a *married pair* is a
   A. train operator's cab   B. storage battery
   C. hand brake   D. door control station

28. Block signals which are normally at danger and which enforce train operation at a predetermined reduced speed are classified as _____ signals.
   A. G.T.   B. S.T.   C. approach   D. dwarf

29. The device which helps to automatically adjust the brake cylinder pressure so that it is in proportion to the car loading is the
   A. equalizing valve   B. inshot valve
   C. slack adjuster   D. variable load valve

30. The device which helps to automatically compensate for the wear of the brake shoes is the
   A. equalizing valve   B. inshot valve
   C. slack adjuster   D. variable load valve

31. Third rail power is used to operate the
   A. compressors   B. emergency car lights
   C. train operator's indication   D. conductor's signal light

32. A train operator should NOT put his hand in the path of the discharge from a carbon dioxide fire extinguisher because the discharge
   A. is a poisonous liquid   B. is very hot
   C. can be re-used   D. can cause frostbite

33. Train operators are cautioned not to use water to extinguish fire near the third rail. The BEST reason for this rule is that water coming into contact with the third rail
   A. causes asphyxiating fumes to be generated
   B. will create a shock hazard
   C. may cause the rail to become rusty
   D. causes poor electrical contact between the shoe and the rail

34. The PREFERRED first-aid treatment for a person who has a badly bleeding forearm is to
   A. apply a splint   B. apply a tourniquet
   C. apply an antiseptic   D. wash with soap and water

35. That part of the brake system which is designed to cause the brakes on all cars in a train to apply equally at the same time is the
   A. equalizing valve   B. dynamic brake
   C. protection reservoir   D. electric brake circuit

36. When operating trains in yards, train operators are instructed to operate from a standing position because, from this position, it is easier to
    A. see the roadway just ahead
    B. manipulate the brake handle
    C. hold down the master controller handle
    D. see the wayside signals

36.____

37. A train operator in the subway can be quite sure that the third rail is dead if the
    A. emergency car lights are dark
    B. doors of the train do not open normally
    C. main car lights are dark and the emergency lights are on
    D. buzzer signals will not sound

37.____

38. If a train operator must move a car with inoperative air brakes from a lay-up track into the shop, he should operate it slowly
    A. using the reverser to stop the car
    B. coupled to a car or cars with good brakes
    C. with a slight hand brake applied
    D. using dynamic brakes

38.____

39. If a train operator has become aware of an acrid odor and arcing while he is operating a train, he should suspect that the trouble is MOST likely to be
    A. a grounded shoe beam
    B. rubbish burning on the tracks
    C. stuck brakes
    D. overloaded traction motors

39.____

40. Besides finding an emergency alarm box at a blue light location in the subway, a train operator would also always find
    A. an emergency exit
    B. flagging lanterns
    C. a telephone
    D. a first-aid kit

40.____

41. An operator could justifiably suspect that the storage batteries of a car were weak if he noticed that the
    A. fans were operating slowly
    B. tail lights were dim
    C. air pressure built up slowly
    D. side destination lights were dim

41.____

42. Safety rules are MOST useful because they
    A. make it unnecessary to think
    B. prevent carelessness
    C. are a guide to avoid common dangers
    D. make the worker responsible for any accident

42.____

43. According to the rules, employees should make no statements about accidents except to proper officials. The PROBABLE reason for this rule is to
    A. conceal facts which may be damaging
    B. prevent unofficial statements from being accepted as official
    C. avoid conflicting testimony
    D. prevent lawsuits

43.____

44. The MOST important reason why train operators are frequently cautioned not to run ahead of schedule is that
    A. the train will have to be held at time points
    B. there is less coasting and more power consumption
    C. employees working on the track may not expect the train so soon
    D. the train behind may become overloaded and delayed

45. The horn signal a train operator or conductor should use when entering a station and they require police assistance is
    A. long-short-long-short
    B. short-short-short-short
    C. long-long-short-short
    D. long-short-short-long

KEY (CORRECT ANSWERS)

1. C	11. B	21. A	31. A	41. B
2. A	12. C	22. C	32. D	42. C
3. A	13. D	23. D	33. B	43. B
4. D	14. B	24. B	34. B	44. D
5. A	15. D	25. D	35. D	45. A
6. B	16. B	26. D	36. A	
7. B	17. D	27. B	37. C	
8. A	18. A	28. A	38. B	
9. C	19. B	29. D	39. A	
10. C	20. D	30. C	40. C	

TEST 3

DIRECTIONS: Each question or incomplete statement is followed by several suggested answers or completions. Select the one that BEST answers the question or completes the statement. *PRINT THE LETTER OF THE CORRECT ANSWER IN THE SPACE AT THE RIGHT.*

1. There is a rapid transit tunnel of the N.Y.C.T.A. under the East River at _____ Street.
   A. Canal   B. 14th   C. 23rd   D. 34th

2. Three principal fixed signal indications are PROCEED, PROCEED WITH CAUTION, and STOP. The PROCEED WITH CAUTION means MOST nearly
   A. go at normal speed for the particular track condition
   B. prepare to stop at next signal
   C. go at not over 20 miles an hour
   D. no need to slow down before reaching the next signal

3. When third rail power fails, one IMMEDIATE effect on a train is that the
   A. ventilating fans cannot operate   B. doors cannot be opened
   C. emergency car lights go out   D. the train whistle is inoperative

4. After cars have been added to a train at a terminal, the brakes must be applied in emergency from the cars which have been added. The purpose of making the brake application from the added cars is to check that
   A. angle cocks are open throughout the entire train
   B. brake valves in both sections that have been coupled are functioning
   C. air compressors on the added cars are working
   D. there is no air leakage at the coupler

5. If a train which has just been coupled parts when taking a *stretch*, the train operator should
   A. recouple at normal speed and take another *stretch*
   B. whistle for a car inspector
   C. get into the other section and couple from there
   D. call the dispatcher for orders

6. The train operator of a local train coasting down the grade between two stations becomes aware of a grounded shoe beam by the severe arcing fumes coming from the shoe beneath his cab. The BEST course of action is to
   A. whistle for a car inspector
   B. stop at the nearest emergency exit and discharge passengers
   C. stop immediately and open the main switch
   D. continue coasting to the next station before taking any other action

2 (#3)

7. When the air brake has been cut out on the last car of a train, the conductor is required to ride in that car to
    A. keep passengers out of the car
    B. operate the doors
    C. flag the train operator of the following train
    D. apply the hand brake if necessary

7.____

8. Before starting out of a terminal, the train operator must
    A. sound the appropriate whistle signal
    B. have a green leaving signal
    C. receive a proceed buzzer signal from the conductor
    D. see the starting lights go on

8.____

Questions 9-12.

DIRECTIONS: Questions 9 through 12, inclusive, in Column I are descriptions of communicating buzzer signal from conductor to train operator, each of which has one of the meanings listed in Column II. For each question in Column I, select the associated meaning from Column II.

Column I

Column II

9. 1 long buzz

A. Start
B. Operator to call for inspector

9.____

10. 2 long buzzes

C. Operator to call for transit police officer

10.____

11. 3 short buzzes

D. Stop

11.____

12. 1 long, 1 short, 1 long, 1 short buzzer signal

12.____

13. The slack adjuster is a device which automatically compensates for the wear of the
    A. brake valves   B. draw bars
    C. brake shoes   D. wheels

13.____

14. One function of the emergency alarm system in the subway is to
    A. provide a means of communication in the event of a power failure
    B. sound a warning to the nearest firehouse
    C. remove power from the third rail
    D. supply power to charge the car batteries

14.____

15. The storage battery on each passenger subway car supplies power for the
    A. main car lights   B. car heaters
    C. tail lights   D. compressors

15.____

16. The devices used in emergencies by train operators to insulate contact shoes from the third rail are known as
    A. slippers   B. fuses   C. insulators   D. transistors

16.____

17. A call-on signal is used only in conjunction with a(n) _____ signal. 17._____
    A. home B. pocket
    C. approach D. dwarf marker

18. A lighted operator's indication informs the train operator that 18._____
    A. the brakes are applied B. all car shoes are making contact
    C. destination signs are lighted D. all side doors are closed

19. A good reason for requiring train operators reporting for duty to read all new bulletin orders is to 19._____
    A. make sure that train operators understand the book of rules
    B. give the dispatcher a chance to observe their condition
    C. acquaint train operators with new regulations
    D. be able to hold train operators responsible for subsequent accidents

Questions 20-25.

DIRECTIONS: Questions 20 through 25, inclusive, are based on the rule immediately preceding the question. Note that more than one question may be based on a given rule. Be sure to consider only the immediately preceding rule in answering each question.

RULE: When moving cars or trains into the shops or inspection sheds, train operators must come to a full stop outside of the shed doors; they must know that doors are fully raised and that cars have safe clearance to pass through; they must blow two distinct blasts of the whistle, then pull into the shed slowly.

20. The train operator must blow two blasts of the whistle in order to 20._____
    A. summon a shop employee to attach the power lead
    B. notify the tower operator to clear the entering signal
    C. warn shop employees of the approach of the train
    D. signal shop employees to open the door

21. According to this rule, on approaching an inspection shed, the train operator must FIRST 21._____
    A. blow two blasts of the whistle
    B. make a full stop
    C. see that the doors are fully raised
    D. check that he has clearance for his entire train

RULE: Employees must give notice in person or by telephone of their intention to be absent from work at least one hour before the time when they should report for duty.

22. This notification of intended absence is required PRIMARILY 22.____
    A. to have time to check the truth of the employee's claim
    B. so that a substitute may be provided if necessary
    C. to complete time records and expedite payrolls
    D. for its nuisance value in limiting absences

RULE: Two yellow lights shall be displayed at a point not less than 500 feet in the approach of the point selected as the flagman's station. One green light shall be displayed a safe distance beyond the farthest point of work.

23. The distance between the flagman and the two yellow lights should be 23.____
    A. 500 feet or more
    B. exactly 500 feet
    C. 500 feet or less
    D. more or less than 500 feet, depending on track conditions

24. A train operator should expect to find a green light 24.____
    A. two or three car lengths past the flagman
    B. a train length past the yellow lights
    C. a train length past the workers on the track
    D. 500 feet past the yellow lights

RULE: Unnecessary blowing of the whistle is forbidden.

25. The MAIN reason for having this rule is that unnecessary blowing of the whistle 25.____
    A. will waste air needed for braking
    B. may cause confusion among passengers on trains
    C. may interfere with the interpretation of necessary signals
    D. will increase the noise in an already noisy place

26. Fixed signals, as described by the book of rules, include _____ signals. 26.____
    A. hand   B. flag   C. repeater   D. whistle

27. A blue light located on the wall of the subway indicates the location of a(n) 27.____
    A. train-order signal   B. fire alarm box
    C. emergency exit   D. telephone

28. Third rail power is used to operate the 28.____
    A. train operator's indication light   B. conductor's signal light
    C. door engines   D. car fluorescent lighting

29. The signals used at congested stations to permit a train to *close in* on a preceding train are called _____ signals.
    A. S.T.   B. G.T.   C. D   D. S

30. The time interval between trains is known as the
    A. layover time
    B. gap
    C. running time
    D. headway

31. The PRINCIPAL cause of accidents is
    A. fatigue
    B. physical disability
    C. carelessness
    D. defective equipment

32. A white light waved up and down by the flagman of a gang of employees working on the track means MOST NEARLY
    A. proceed with caution to the green lantern
    B. pull up to me, I have a message for you
    C. your whistle signal has been heard; stop and wait for proceed signal
    D. resume normal speed; I'm in the clear

33. After applying the required number of hand brakes on a train which has been laid up on a steep grade, the PROPER test of whether the hand brakes will hold the train is to
    A. examine each hand brake chain to see that it is tight
    B. apply the brakes in emergency
    C. open the compressor switches
    D. place a brake valve in release

34. A train operator should operate their train safely at all times but should also try to maintain the schedule. This can BEST be done by
    A. following the rules intelligently
    B. using his best judgment regardless of the rules
    C. disregarding the less important rules when necessary
    D. obeying the rules to the letter

35. An train operator on the transit system knows that if one shoe of a subway car is touching the third rail, the number of shoes alive on that car is
    A. one   B. two   C. three   D. four

KEY (CORRECT ANSWERS)

1.	B	11.	B	21.	B	31.	C
2.	B	12.	C	22.	B	32.	A
3.	A	13.	C	23.	A	33.	D
4.	A	14.	C	24.	C	34.	A
5.	A	15.	C	25.	C	35.	D
6.	D	16.	A	26.	C		
7.	D	17.	A	27.	D		
8.	C	18.	D	28.	D		
9.	D	19.	C	29.	A		
10.	A	20.	C	30.	D		

TEST 4

DIRECTIONS: Each question or incomplete statement is followed by several suggested answers or completions. Select the one that BEST answers the question or completes the statement. *PRINT THE LETTER OF THE CORRECT ANSWER IN THE SPACE AT THE RIGHT.*

1. A bulletin states that the crew of a train which is stalled should make every effort to obtain information concerning the cause of the delay and should announce to passengers the cause and probable duration. The MAIN reason for making the announcement is to
    A. help clear up the trouble
    B. show that transit employees know their job
    C. keep the train crew occupied
    D. avoid confusion and apprehension among passengers

    1.____

2. When it is necessary for a train operator to pull an emergency alarm, the rules state that he MUST then immediately notify the
    A. transit police
    B. rail control center
    C. fire department
    D. terminal dispatcher

    2.____

3. If a train is tripped while running at about 18 miles per hour, the MOST serious consequence to the equipment will probably be
    A. worn brake shoes
    B. hot journal boxes
    C. locked brakes
    D. flat wheels

    3.____

4. In the interest of safety, a train operator should NOT
    A. move his train past a stop arm that is hooked down
    B. try to make up lost time
    C. accept a PROCEED hand signal from a signal maintainer in the face of a red over red signal
    D. center the reverser with the train in motion

    4.____

5. A bulletin states that it is permissible for conductors to remove their uniform coats while on duty during a specified part of the year. It would be logical to conclude that the part of the year specified is from
    A. February 1st to May 1st
    B. May 1st to October 1st
    C. October 1st to December 1st
    D. December 1st to February 1st

    5.____

6. At transfer points, it is especially desirable that trains make *meets*
    A. at all times
    B. at noontime
    C. during rush hours
    D. late at night

    6.____

7. The *electric portion* is part of the
    A. master controller
    B. door engine
    C. electro-pneumatic brake
    D. coupler

    7.____

8. An operator should use the route request button that is installed at an interlocking home signal when
   A. the signal indicates stop
   B. a call-on is displayed
   C. the signal indicates proceed on main line
   D. signal indicates proceed on diverging route

8.____

9. The MAIN reason operators are requested to coast as much as possible consistent with keeping on schedule is that coasting reduces
   A. contact shoe wear
   B. power consumption
   C. wheel maintenance
   D. brake shoe wear

9.____

10. Before moving a train in a yard, it is MOST important for a train operator to check the
    A. couplers
    B. brakes
    C. drum switches
    D. train whistle

10.____

Questions 11-20.

DIRECTIONS: Questions 11 through 20, inclusive, are based on passenger cars older than R-10 cars; these cars are equipped with ME-23 brake valves.

11. The normal position of the operating brake valve when running over the road should be
    A. service   B. handle-off   C. lap   D. release

11.____

12. The normal position of a non-operating brake valve is
    A. release   B. lap   C. handle-off   D. service

12.____

13. With the brake handle in the extreme left position, the valve is in
    A. service   B. emergency   C. release   D. handle-off

13.____

14. The normal reading of the black hand of the duplex air gauge should be APPROXIMATELY _____ pounds.
    A. 60   B. 70   C. 80   D. 90

14.____

15. The air pressure in the train air brake system will be reduced to zero if all the
    A. double cut-out cocks are opened
    B. brake valves are set in service position
    C. main reservoir drain cocks are left closed
    D. main reservoir drain cocks are left open

15.____

16. To make an emergency stop when the electric feature of the electro-pneumatic brake system is operating properly, the train operator should place the brake handle in the emergency position and then
    A. quickly move it to release
    B. leave it there until the train slows down and then move it to lap
    C. leave it there until the train stops
    D. quickly move it to electric holding

17. The positions of the brake valve which are normally used when graduating off the brakes are
    A. electric holding and lap
    B. handle-off and release
    C. release and electric holding
    D. service and handle-off

18. The normal reading of the red hand of the duplex air gauge should be APPROXIMATELY _____ pounds.
    A. 60
    B. 70
    C. 80
    D. 90

19. If the brakes go into emergency from an unknown cause, the train operator should IMMEDIATELY lap his brake handle to
    A. bring the train to a smoother stop
    B. prevent the brakes from locking
    C. prevent the *dead-man* feature from operating
    D. aid in discovering the cause

20. The brakes do NOT apply in emergency when cars are properly uncoupled because the _____ on both cars.
    A. brake valve is in lap
    B. brake pipe is closed
    C. brake pipe is temporarily overcharged
    D. UE-5 valve is in lap

Questions 21-30.

DIRECTIONS: Questions 21 through 30, inclusive, are based on the R-10 or later type passenger cars equipped with ME-42 brake valves.

21. When the brake valve handle is in its extreme right-hand position, the brake valve is in
    A. full release
    B. handle-off
    C. full service
    D. running release

22. The normal position of the operating brake valve when running over the road is
    A. handle-off
    B. running release
    C. full service
    D. full release

23. The normal position of a non-operating brake valve is
    A. full release
    B. full service
    C. running release
    D. handle-off

4 (#4)

24. The dynamic brakes will NOT start to function until the train has reached a speed of _____ MPH
    A. 5   B. 10   C. 15   D. 20

25. The normal main reservoir pressure is in the range of _____ lbs.
    A. 155 to 190   B. 125 to 150   C. 105 to 120   D. 85 to 100

26. The black hand on the duplex air gauge indicates the pressure in the
    A. brake pipe
    B. compressor
    C. straight air pipe
    D. main reservoir

27. The red hand on the duplex air gauge indicates the pressure in the
    A. main reservoir
    B. straight air pipe
    C. compressor
    D. brake pipe

28. The reading of the black hand of the duplex air gauge when operating normally should be APPROXIMATELY _____ lbs.
    A. 110   B. 80   C. 60   D. 0

29. The reading of the red hand of the duplex air gauge when operating normally should be _____ lbs.
    A. 0   B. 60   C. 80   D. 110

30. All cars later than the R-10 series are equipped with door relays. The function of the door relay is to
    A. prevent opening of doors on the wrong side of the train at a station
    B. permit operation of all doors in the train from one control point
    C. apply the brakes if a door opens while the train is in motion
    D. close the control circuit after all doors are closed

Questions 31-46.

DIRECTIONS: Questions 31 through 46, inclusive, are based on the accompanying illustrations of color-light signals, signs, and markers used on the transit system. A pair of illustrations is given when necessary to show two aspects having the same meaning. In the illustrations, the colors are illuminated signs, S denotes an illuminated S sign, and W denotes auxiliary white lens illuminated.

31. This signal tells a train operator to
    A. stop, then key-by
    B. proceed with caution
    C. do not exceed series speed
    D. stop and stay

32. This signal means
    A. stop and stay
    B. operate at not over 10 MPH
    C. proceed with caution
    D. stop, then key-by

33. After passing this sign, the train operator MUST
    A. blow two blasts of the whistle
    B. operate without signal indications
    C. stop and telephone for orders
    D. operate at not over series speed

34. This sign means ten-car
    A. train has cleared crossover
    B. trains start coasting here
    C. trains stop here when making turning move
    D. trains stop here for station shop

35. This signal aspect means
    A. proceed slowly
    B. stop and stay
    C. stop, then key-by
    D. proceed with caution at allowable speed

36. This signal indicates
    A. prepare to stop at next signal
    B. proceed
    C. preceding train may be only four blocks ahead
    D. proceed at indicated speed

37. This sign indicates ten-car
    A. trains stop here when making turning move
    B. trains stop here for station stop
    C. train has cleared crossover
    D. trains start coasting here

38. At this sign, the train operator of a ten-car train should
    A. stop to make a reverse move
    B. remove power from the motors
    C. resume normal operation
    D. make a station stop

39. This signal means proceed
    A. normally on main route
    B. with caution on main route
    C. normally on diverging route
    D. with caution on diverging route

39._____

40. The signal aspect shown means
    A. stop and stay
    B. stop and telephone the dispatcher's office
    C. stop and blow whistle for a change of route
    D. stop, then key-by

40._____

41. The train operator observing this aspect may
    A. proceed on diverging route expecting next signal to be yellow or green
    B. resume speed after taking crossover
    C. proceed on main route expecting next signal to be yellow or green
    D. proceed over crossover at indicated speed

41._____

42. This signal means proceed with
    A. caution on diverging route
    B. no speed restriction on diverging route
    C. caution on main route
    D. no speed restriction on main route

42.____

43. The indication of this signal is
    A. stop, operate stop release, then proceed with caution prepared to stop
    B. stop, then take siding or enter yard lead
    C. stop and signal tower for a change of route
    D. stop and stay

43.____

44. This signal requires the train operator to
    A. stop, operate stop release, then proceed with caution prepared to stop
    B. stop and blow for a change of route
    C. proceed with caution on to yard lead or siding
    D. enter inspection shed prepared to stop within vision

44.____

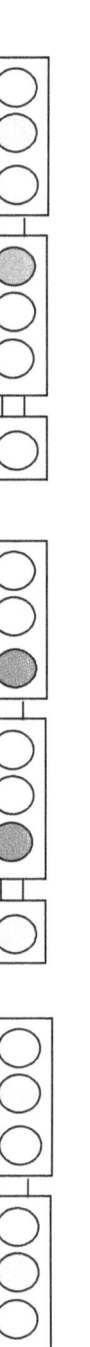

45. This signal aspect means proceed
    A. on diverging route
    B. on main route
    C. with caution on diverging route
    D. with caution on main route

45.____

46. This sign requires a train operator to
    A. reduce speed to 10 MPH for diverging route
    B. take siding at 10 MPH
    C. approach time-controlled signals at 10 MPH
    D. approach bumper at 10 MPH

46.____

47. If seven ten-car trains and eight eight-car trains pass a point on a certain track during one hour, the headway on that track is _____ minutes.
    A. 3   B. 4   C. 5   D. 6

47.____

48. If the average speed of a train is 30 miles per hour, the time it takes the train to travel one mile is _____ minutes.
    A. 2   B. 3   C. 4   D. 5

48.____

49. A trailing point switch is a switch the points of which
    A. face approaching traffic
    B. make up against the face of the rail
    C. face in the direction of traffic flow
    D. face the tower

49.____

50. A train operator bypasses a station without permission. The responsibility of the conductor by rule is to
    A. immediately engage the emergency break valve and contact the rail control center
    B. wait until the train is safely in the next station and then engage the emergency brake valve so passengers are not injured
    C. immediately contact your train operator to ensure they are okay and then engage the emergency brake valve before calling the rail control center
    D. immediately contact the rail control center and safely follow their instructions

50.____

KEY (CORRECT ANSWERS)

1.	D	11.	D	21.	B	31.	B	41.	C
2.	B	12.	C	22.	B	32.	D	42.	C
3.	D	13.	C	23.	D	33.	B	43.	A
4.	D	14.	B	24.	C	34.	C	44.	C
5.	B	15.	D	25.	B	35.	D	45.	A
6.	D	16.	C	26.	A	36.	B	46.	C
7.	D	17.	C	27.	B	37.	B	47.	B
8.	A	18.	D	28.	A	38.	C	48.	A
9.	B	19.	D	29.	A	39.	D	49.	C
10.	B	20.	B	30.	D	40.	A	50.	A

TEST 5

DIRECTIONS: Each question or incomplete statement is followed by several suggested answers or completions. Select the one that BEST answers the question or completes the statement. *PRINT THE LETTER OF THE CORRECT ANSWER IN THE SPACE AT THE RIGHT.*

1. The automatic stop manual release is used MAINLY in conjunction with _____ signals. 1.____
   A. home   B. approach   C. automatic   D. dwarf

2. The position of the master controller that must NEVER be used as a running position is 2.____
   A. off   B. switching   C. series   D. multiple

3. The operator of an express train notices that the operator's indication light is out when the train is in motion about midway between subway express stations. According to the most recent regulation, his FIRST action must be to 3.____
   A. whistle for the car inspector
   B. sound the buzzer for the conductor
   C. bring the train to a stop
   D. operate the reset switch

4. When power has been off the third rail and is subsequently restored, train operators of passenger trains are required to 4.____
   A. call the trainmaster before starting up
   B. make a stop of one full minute at the first station
   C. operate in series speed for the first two minutes
   D. operate in switching speed for one minute

5. A bulletin order specifies that certain trains must be keyed 1-4-4-1. This means that the 5.____
   A. train will be double-ended for an unusual movement
   B. door controls must be set up for two-conductor operation
   C. train must be set up for quick cutting into two five-car units
   D. main light controls must be set up for operation from four locations

6. When a train operator observes two yellow caution lanterns displayed adjacent to the track in the subway, he MUST signal with the train whistle by blowing _____ short blast(s). 6.____
   A. one   B. two   C. three   D. four

7. In addition to blowing the required whistle signal, the operator of the train in Question 6 above is required by the rules to 7.____
   A. make an emergency stop
   B. make a service stop
   C. place the master controller in series
   D. bring train speed down to 10 MPH

2 (#5)

8. If, in response to his whistle signal, the train operator in Question 6 above observes a white light being moved rapidly up and down, he will be observing the rules if he promptly
   A. resumes normal operation
   B. places his master controller in series
   C. blows two short blasts of the train whistle
   D. applies brakes to stop at the light

8.____

9. If there is an unattended white light on the benchwalk adjacent to his track in the subway, the train operator observing this is required to
   A. stop and investigate, then report to the rail control center
   B. pass at slow speed until sure that no one is on the tracks
   C. continue at normal speed and report it at the first open tower
   D. stop and pick up the light and turn it in at the terminal

9.____

10. The MAXIMUM speed permitted by the rules on curved tracks in yards is
    A. 5 MPH   B. 10 MPH   C. 15 MPH   D. series speed

10.____

11. The MAXIMUM speed permitted by the rules when a train is passing through a passenger station without stopping is
    A. 5 MPH   B. 10 MPH   C. 15 MPH   D. series speed

11.____

12. Operators operating trains in the subway or open cuts are forbidden to pass a location where water has accumulated to the ball of the running rail. The depth of water over the ties at such a time is CLOSEST to _____ inches.
    A. 3   B. 6   C. 12   D. 24

12.____

13. The designation which does NOT refer to a subway car coupler is
    A. H2A   B. H2C   C. J1   D. AC

13.____

14. If a train operator notices a white light being waved to and fro on the track ahead of his moving train, he knows it is a signal for him to
    A. slow down and stop
    B. test his brakes
    C. pass the signal light at reduced speed
    D. proceed at normal speed

14.____

15. Under certain conditions, a train operator is forbidden by rule to start his train until, in addition to the train operator's starting light, he also receives a buzzer signal. Such buzzer signal is NOT required when starting
    A. from a terminal
    B. after cars have been cut or added
    C. after an emergency stop
    D. from a regular station stop

15.____

16. A train is said to have developed a grounded shoe beam when the wooden beam which carries the shoe 16.____
    A. becomes loose and drags on the ground
    B. breaks off and falls to the ground
    C. breaks down and becomes an electrical conductor
    D. carries insufficient electrical current to active the train controls

17. At a blue light location in the subway, there is USUALLY an emergency 17.____
    A. exit and fire extinguisher
    B. exit and an emergency alarm box
    C. telephone and a home signal
    D. telephone and an emergency alarm box

18. Train operators generally know the points at which coasting is required under normal operating conditions by 18.____
    A. judgment gained through experience
    B. bulletins posted at their home terminals
    C. oral instructions from the train operator instructor or dispatcher
    D. signs along the route

19. The PROPER whistle signal to warn people standing near the edge of the platform is 19.____
    A. any signal that may be convenient
    B. two long blasts
    C. two short blasts
    D. an unspecified number of short blasts

Questions 20-32.

DIRECTIONS: Questions 20 through 32, inclusive, are each based on the rule immediately preceding the question. Note that more than one question may be based on a given rule. Be sure to consider only the immediately preceding rule in answering each question.

RULE: In rainy weather, while moving cars in yards, a stop must be made at least three car lengths from shop doors, standing cars, or bumping blocks; then proceed very slowly.

20. The reason for the mandatory stop is that, in rainy weather, 20.____
    A. visibility is low   B. brakes do not hold well
    C. yard tracks may be slippery   D. there is likely to be more arcing

21. The distance of the stop from the bumping block, cars, or shop doors is easily estimated to be CLOSEST to _____ feet. 21.____
    A. 90   B. 180   C. 360   D. 600

RULE: During daylight hours, conductors of trains equipped with remote control of car body lights will extinguish the lights while the train is operating in the open; it will not be necessary to do this when the running time between two portals is five minutes or less.

22. One location where car body lights need NOT be extinguished during daylight hours is 22.____
    A. Hudson Street to Rockaway Park on the Rockaway Line
    B. Ditmas Avenue to Stillwell Avenue on the Culver Line
    C. Marcy Avenue to 168th Street on the Jamaica Line
    D. 116th Street to 137th Street on the Van Cortlandt Park Line

RULE: When coupling cars, be sure couplers are properly aligned, electric portion slides fully retrieved, and shutters closed. From a point approximately two feet from cars to which coupling is to be made, bring cars together at a speed of one mile an hour. After coupling is made, brake valve handle must be placed in *full service* position to automatically unlock the electric portion slide and fully charge the brake pipe system. Safety chains must be hung in operating position. When making coupling on a grade, move cars upgrade.

23. The coupling speed specified is equivalent to about one and one-half 23.____
    A. feet per minute   B. feet per second
    C. minutes per foot   D. seconds per foot

24. One important reason that the electric portion slides MUST be fully retrieved before coupling is to be sure that 24.____
    A. mechanical coupling is completed before electrical connections are made
    B. air connections are properly set up to permit the coupling
    C. electrical connections are properly set up to permit the coupling
    D. coupler heads are free so they can be properly aligned for coupling

25. One location where the operating position of the safety chains is different from the operating position at MOST other locations is 25.____
    A. at the conductor's station
    B. midway between the conductor's station and the rear of the train
    C. midway between the conductor's position and the front of the train
    D. at the front of the train and rear of the train

26. The PRINCIPAL safety feature realized by coupling upgrade is that the 26.____
    A. impact is less
    B. coupler on the stationary section is centered because it hangs downgrade
    C. stationary cars cannot accidentally roll away if the coupling fails to make
    D. hand brakes do not have to be set up on the stationary section before coupling

RULE: Operators operating trains which have been rerouted over other than normal track will, upon arriving at subsequent interlockings, use the route request button for return to normal track. If, after using the route request button, the alternate route continues to be displayed, the train operator will accept same, providing the alternate route will enable him to continue on his designated line and return to his normal track at a subsequent interlocking. If the route displayed will require the train operator to operate over other than scheduled line, he must obtain permission from the rain control center, either directly or through the tower operator, to accept same.

27. The signal indicating the alternate route would PROBABLY display the aspect
    A. green over green
    B. yellow over yellow over yellow
    C. yellow over illuminated S
    D. red over red over yellow

28. If the alternate route permits no return to original destination and the response to the route request is a flashing of the signal to STOP and then back to the alternate route aspect, the train operator must
    A. contact the rail control center
    B. accept the alternate route
    C. repeat his request
    D. use the other route request button

29. The route request buttons are generally located at home signals. One condition which may require that there be duplicate route request buttons at several locations in approach to a particular home signals is when the home signal is at the
    A. leaving end of a station
    B. entering end of a station
    C. portal entering a yard
    D. portal leaving a yard

RULE: When a work train is positioned at a work area and power is to removed, the train must be properly secured by a sufficient number of hand brakes. The train operator must also cut out the entire train, including battery switches.

30. Hand brakes MUST be applied because the air brakes
    A. are automatically cut out when power is removed
    B. may leak off since the compressors are inoperative
    C. do not hold a train as firmly as the hand brakes do
    D. can be released at the wrong time by an unauthorized person

31. The battery switches are cut out PRIMARILY to
    A. prevent unauthorized starting of the train
    B. retain battery charge
    C. protect battery-operated equipment
    D. prevent loss of air

RULE: Train operators operating light or work trains over open structure will not sound whistle between dusk and dawn unless the train is involved in a reverse movement.

32. The LOGICAL reason for this rule is to avoid noise that may be objectionable to
    A. police   B. firemen   C. residents   D. maintainers

33. With respect to the movement of traffic over it, the switch sketched at the right is PROPERLY called a
    A. single slip
    B. facing-point
    C. trailing-point
    D. double slip

34. If a train moved over the switch in Question 33 above in the direction of traffic from point 2 to 3, but the switch was aligned for the move from point 1 to 3, it can PROPERLY be said that the train _____ the switch.
    A. split   B. ran through   C. opened   D. closed

35. One step in making the brake test at a terminal or yard is to release the master controller handle and allow the brakes to apply in emergency. The MAIN purpose of this step is to
    A. check the continuity of the brake pipe
    B. test the operation of the dead-man feature
    C. be sure the brakes are operative on all cars
    D. test operation of the air compressors

36. If only one shoe of a car is on the third rail, the other
    A. three shoes will be dead
    B. three shoes will be alive
    C. shoe on the same track will be alive and the shoes on the other truck will be dead
    D. shoe on the same side of the car will be alive, and the remaining two shoes will be dead

37. A red lantern on the rear of a car on a yard lay-up track is an indication that
    A. the air brake is inoperative
    B. workers are on or beneath the car
    C. all cab switches have been cut out
    D. the car is up against the bumper

38. When making a report of an unusual occurrence on a train in the subway, it is LEAST important to include the
    A. date
    B. time of day
    C. number of car in the train
    D. number of the car in which the occurrence took place

39. It sometimes becomes necessary to move a car having inoperative air brakes from a storage track in a yard to a track in the shop. The PROPER way to make such a movement is to
    A. couple the defective car to one or more cars having good brakes
    B. have two train operators on the car, one to handle the controller and one the hand brake
    C. set the hand brake 90% on and then run very slowly
    D. operate with a light hand brake set up, reversing the motors to stop

40. The Department of Subways Service Delivery is part of what MTA Division?
    A. RTD – Rapid Transit Department
    B. RTO – Rapid Transit Operations
    C. CSM – Customer Service Movement
    D. SSO – Subway Safety Operations

KEY (CORRECT ANSWERS)

1.	A	11.	C	21.	B	31.	B
2.	B	12.	B	22.	D	32.	C
3.	C	13.	D	23.	B	33.	C
4.	C	14.	A	24.	A	34.	B
5.	B	15.	D	25.	D	35.	B
6.	B	16.	C	26.	C	36.	B
7.	D	17.	D	27.	A	37.	B
8.	C	18.	D	28.	A	38.	C
9.	A	19.	D	29.	A	39.	A
10.	B	20.	C	30.	B	40.	B

EXAMINATION SECTION
TEST 1

DIRECTIONS: Each question or incomplete statement is followed by several suggested answers or completions. Select the one that BEST answers the question or completes the statement. *PRINT THE LETTER OF THE CORRECT ANSWER IN THE SPACE AT THE RIGHT.*

1. If the train whistle becomes inoperative enroute, the train operator should
   A. stop immediately and call the rail control center for orders
   B. operate from the second car
   C. have the conductor blow the whistle when necessary from the cab in his car
   D. proceed cautiously and report the condition at the first opportunity

2. The time when it is LEAST important for local and express trains to make *meets* at transfer points is
   A. late at night
   B. during rush hours
   C. Sunday mornings
   D. Saturday afternoons

3. The round trip time between two terminals, not including layover time, is 1 hour, 20 minutes. A train due to arrive at one terminal at 9:10 should leave the other terminal at
   A. 7:50   B. 8:00   C. 8:10   D. 8:30

4. An express train requires five minutes to make the run between two stations which are two and one-half miles apart. The average speed of the train for this run is _____ MPH.
   A. 24   B. 30   C. 36   D. 42

5. If twenty ten-car trains and ten eight-car trains pass a point on a certain track during one hour, the headway on that track, in minutes, is
   A. 1½   B. 2   C. 3   D. 6

6. One purpose of the electric brake circuit is to
   A. prevent accidental emergency application
   B. apply the brakes equally on all cars at the same time
   C. ensure a smooth final stop under all operating conditions
   D. start all compressors at the same time

7. The signals used at congested stations to permit a train to close in on the train ahead are called _____ signals.
   A. G.T.   B. A.K.   C. S.T.   D. C.I.

8. If a stranger starts to question you about an accident which occurred on the subway, your BEST action in accordance with the rules is to
   A. say "no comment"
   B. ask him for his credentials
   C. refer him to the Transit Authority
   D. answer those questions about which you have first-hand information

9. The assistant dispatcher at a time point requests a train operator to whistle for the signal maintainer when he reaches a particular area. The train operator should
   A. call the rail control center for verification
   B. ask the assistant dispatcher for written authorization
   C. tell the assistant dispatcher that it is a rule violation
   D. acknowledge the request and carry it out

10. Pulling the emergency cord on a subway car
    A. opens an air valve
    B. opens a switch
    C. closes an air valve
    D. closes a switch

11. A passenger on the street at Borough Hall, Brooklyn, requests information as to the most direct means of reaching Herald Square (Broadway and 34th Street, Manhattan). You should tell him to use the _____ Line.
    A. 4th Avenue F train at Jay Street
    B. 7th Avenue
    C. Lexington Avenue
    D. Washington Heights

12. If the electric feature of the electro-pneumatic brake fails to function properly on a moving train, the MOST likely result would be that the train will
    A. make a normal stop when the train operator makes a normal brake application
    B. make an emergency stop when the train operator makes a normal brake application
    C. stop beyond the usual stop when the train operator makes a normal brake application
    D. make a normal stop only if the train operator makes an emergency brake application

13. There is NO rapid transit tunnel under the East River at _____ Street.
    A. 14th   B. 42nd   C. 53rd   D. 67th

14. After coasting for some distance, a train operator on a regular subway run moves the controller handle to multiple and finds that the train does not pick up speed. They CANNOT find out whether the third rail is dead by
    A. turning on the heaters
    B. observing the main car lighting
    C. blowing the train whistle
    D. turning on the fans

15. When operating trains in yards, train operators are instructed to operate from a standing position because, from this position, it is easier to
    A. see anyone near or approaching the track
    B. hold down the handle of the master controller
    C. manipulate the brake handle
    D. see further down the track

16. The Lost and Found Office of the N.Y.C.T.A. is located at
    A. 25 Jamaica Avenue   B. 3961 10th Avenue
    C. 370 Jay Street   D. 73 Rockwell Place

17. According to the rules, an employee discovering an incipient fire shall exercise all means in his power to extinguish the fire promptly. An incipient fire means a fire which
    A. is near the third rail   B. is easy to extinguish
    C. seems to be spreading rapidly   D. has just started

18. A train operator would be acting in violation of the rules if he
    A. sounded five short blasts of the whistle when skipping a regular passenger station
    B. refused a request to make an extra run after his regular tour
    C. absented himself from duty because of illness
    D. coasted between stations with his reverser centered

19. A train operator taking a lay-up train to the yard, and following a regular passenger train enroute, MUST be especially careful to
    A. follow the train ahead as closely as signals permit
    B. remain outside each passenger station until he can get his entire train beyond it
    C. give the train ahead as much headway as possible without delaying the train behind
    D. keep his speed below 10 MPH at all times

Questions 20-27.

DIRECTIONS: Questions 20 through 27, inclusive, are based on the R-10 or later type passenger cars equipped with ME-42 brake valves.

20. The normal main reservoir pressure is in the range of _____ lbs.
    A. 90 to 105   B. 110 to 120   C. 125 to 150   D. 160 to 180

21. The red hand on the duplex air gage indicates the pressure in the
    A. straight air pipe   B. brake pipe
    C. brake cylinder   D. compressor

22. The pressure in the main reservoir is indicated
    A. by the setting of the feed valve
    B. on a gage under one of the seats
    C. on a gage under the car
    D. by the setting of the compressor governor

23. While running in normal service, the red hand of the duplex air gage should read
    A. 0   B. 70   C. 90   D. 110

24. While running in normal service, the black hand of the duplex air gage should read
    A. 0   B. 70   C. 90   D. 110

25. On a properly maintained train, an emergency stop will NOT always result from
    A. operation of the conductor's valve
    B. tripping by an automatic stop
    C. release of the controller handle
    D. rapid decrease in brake pipe pressure

26. Dynamic brakes help the electro-pneumatic brake bring a train to a stop by
    A. allowing the use of larger brake shoes
    B. using a separate set of brake drums
    C. magnetizing the brake shoes
    D. having the driving motors act as a braking force

27. The battery on a train furnishes energy to operate (among other items) the group switches which control the third rail power fed to the main motors. A logical consequence of low battery voltage is, therefore, that
    A. the train may be slow
    B. there may not be enough braking power
    C. arcing may become excessive
    D. the operator may have to notch up the controller by hand

Questions 28-40.

DIRECTIONS: Questions 28 through 40, inclusive, are based on the accompanying illustrations of color-light signals, signs, and markers used on the transit system. A pair of illustrations is given when necessary to show two aspects having the same meaning. In the accompanying illustrations, S denotes an illuminated S sign and W denotes auxiliary white lens illuminated.

28. The indication of this signal is
    A. proceed with caution
    B. stop and then proceed, prepared to stop within vision
    C. proceed with caution at allowable speed
    D. proceed

29. This signal means
    A. proceed with caution
    B. stop and then proceed, prepared to stop within vision
    C. proceed with caution at allowable speed
    D. proceed expecting to find track occupied

29._____

30. This signal indicates
    A. stop and stay
    B. stop and then proceed, prepared to stop within vision
    C. proceed with caution at allowable speed
    D. proceed with caution

30._____

31. The indication of this illuminated sign is
    A. beginning of time control at indicated speed
    B. speed restricted to indicated speed on curve
    C. take turnout at indicated speed
    D. approaching a terminal, maintain indicated speed

31._____

32. This sign means that
    A. there are no speed restrictions beyond this point
    B. you have just passed a length of track signaled for both directions
    C. you have just passed out of interlocking control
    D. block signaling ends at this point

32._____

33. This illuminated sign is used as the
    A. station stop marker for 8-car trains
    B. turning point marker for 8-car trains
    C. indication that coasting for an 8-car train should begin here
    D. indication that the rear of an 8-car train is past a crossover

33._____

34. This signal aspect means that a train operator may
    A. proceed normally on either route
    B. proceed at not exceeding 25 MPH on main route
    C. proceed normally on diverging route
    D. proceed on main route expecting next signal to be clear

35. This signal aspect means that a train operator may proceed on
    A. diverging route expecting next signal to be red
    B. main route expecting next signal to be red
    C. diverging route expecting next signal to be clear
    D. main route expecting next signal to be clear

36. This signal indicates
    A. stop and blow four short blasts
    B. stop, operate stop release, then proceed with caution
    C. stop and stay until a less restrictive aspect appears
    D. stop and telephone for orders

37. This signal aspect means that an operator may proceed on
    A. diverging route expecting next signal to be red
    B. main route expecting next signal to be red
    C. diverging route expecting next signal to be clear
    D. main route expecting next signal to be clear

37._____

38. The indication shown is proceed
    A. on main route
    B. with caution on diverging route
    C. on diverging route
    D. with caution on main route

38._____

39. The aspect shown means
    A. stop and blow whistle for route
    B. stop, operate stop release, then proceed within vision
    C. stop and stay until a less restrictive aspect appears
    D. stop and telephone for orders

39._____

40. The indication shown would MOST probably permit a train operator to
    A. operate the stop release and then proceed with caution
    B. operate the hand throw switch and then proceed with caution
    C. enter inspection shed with caution
    D. proceed with caution onto yard lead

40.____

KEY (CORRECT ANSWERS)

1.	A	11.	A	21.	A	31.	A
2.	B	12.	C	22.	C	32.	D
3.	D	13.	D	23.	A	33.	D
4.	B	14.	C	24.	D	34.	D
5.	B	15.	A	25.	C	35.	A
6.	B	16.	C	26.	D	36.	C
7.	C	17.	D	27.	A	37.	C
8.	C	18.	D	28.	D	38.	D
9.	D	19.	B	29.	A	39.	B
10.	A	20.	C	30.	C	40.	D

TEST 2

DIRECTIONS: Each question or incomplete statement is followed by several suggested answers or completions. Select the one that BEST answers the question or completes the statement. *PRINT THE LETTER OF THE CORRECT ANSWER IN THE SPACE AT THE RIGHT.*

1. An IMPORTANT safety concept for a train operator to bear in mind is that 1.____
   A. some accidents are unavoidable if the schedule is to be maintained
   B. according to the law of averages, a certain number of accidents will occur each year
   C. some train operators are more apt to have accidents than others
   D. most accidents can be avoided if proper precautions are taken

2. If a train operator has a poor accident record, it would be logical to assume that the train operator is PROBABLY 2.____
   A. unlucky   B. careless
   C. overcautious   D. safety conscious

3. Artificial respiration should be started immediately on a train operator who has suffered an electric shock by coming in contact with the third rail if he is 3.____
   A. unconscious and breathing heavily
   B. unconscious and not breathing
   C. conscious and in a daze
   D. conscious and badly burned

4. The black hand of the duplex air gage on any type of car indicates the air pressure in the 4.____
   A. brake pipe   B. straight air pipe
   C. main air line   D. brake cylinder

5. At blue light locations in the subway, a train operator would expect to find both 5.____
   A. emergency alarms and emergency exits
   B. telephones and first aid kits
   C. fire extinguishers and stretchers
   D. telephones and fire extinguishers

6. The SAFEST assumption for a train operator to make when he receives a proceed buzzer signal but his indication light remains dark is that 6.____
   A. all side doors are closed   B. the indication lamp has burned out
   C. the indication circuit is defective   D. a side door is open

7. When coupling cars, they should be brought together at a speed of about _____ MPH. 7.____
   A. ¼   B. 1   C. 4   D. 7

119

2 (#2)

8. If the headway on a certain track is 5 minutes, the number of trains per hour on that track is
   A. 15 B. 14 C. 12 D. 10

9. If the average speed of a train is 30 miles per hour, the time it takes the train to travel one mile is _____ minute(s).
   A. 1 B. 2 C. 3 D. 4

10. A five-track lay-up yard can hold a total of five ten-car trains. There are already three cars stored on each of four tracks and four cars stored on the fifth track. The number of additional cars that can be stored in this yard is
    A. 14 B. 24 C. 34 D. 44

11. A train operator stops his local train at a home signal indicating Stop. If his train is on an upgrade, the train operator should
    A. apply a light-hand stroke
    B. keep his full service brake applied
    C. graduate off the air brake until the train just begins to roll
    D. apply the brakes in emergency

12. An empty train bound for the yard is halted at a stop signal outside a station occupied by a regular passenger train. According to the rules, the train operator of the empty train should start entering the station
    A. as soon as it is safe to key by the stop signal
    B. as soon as the regular passenger train starts to move
    C. when he is sure to be able to get his entire train into the station
    D. when he is sure to be able to get his entire train past the station

13. Operation of the brake on the latest type of car in use on the transit system has been said to be similar to operation of the brake on an automobile. The GREATEST similarity lies in the fact that
    A. hydraulic brakes are used on both trains and automobiles
    B. the greater the motion of the brake handle or pedal, the harder the brake is applied
    C. both trains and automobiles have foot-operated brakes and hand brakes
    D. there is an individual brake cylinder for each pair of wheels

14. Contact shoe slippers must NOT be used when wet because a wet contact shoe slipper
    A. may adhere to the shoe, causing arcing
    B. is likely to break more easily than a dry one
    C. is not a good insulator, so the user may receive a shock
    D. may wear away rapidly because it is soft

15. To avoid a serious arc, a third rail emergency jumper should NOT be removed from the third rail or shoe until the
    A. main switch is open
    B. shoe is off the third rail
    C. car is in motion
    D. master controller is in the off position

16. In certain equipment failures it becomes necessary for the operator of a passenger train to operate from the second car with the conductor at the head end to pass back signals via the buzzer. In such cases, the crew is required to discharge passengers at the next station. The BEST reason for discharge of passengers in such cases is that
    A. carrying passengers under these conditions would cause extreme delays
    B. it is not possible to operate safely
    C. incorrect markers are automatically displayed
    D. the train operator cannot see the station stop markers

Questions 17-21.

DIRECTIONS: Questions 17 through 21, inclusive, are based on the notice given below. Refer to this notice in answering these questions.

NOTICE

Your attention is called to Route Request Buttons that are installed on all new type interlocking home signals where there is a choice of route in the midtown area. The route request button is to be operated by the train operator when the home signal is at danger and no call-on is displayed or when improper route is displayed.

To operate, the train operator will press the button for the desired route as indicated under each button; a light will then go on over the buttons to inform the train operator that his request has been registered in the tower.

If the tower operator desires to give the train operator a route other than the one he selected, the tower operator will cancel out the light over the route selection buttons. The train operator will then accept the route given.

If no route or call-on is given, the operator will sound his whistle for the signal maintainer, secure his train, and call the rail control center.

17. The official titles of the two classes of employee whose actions would MOST frequently be affected by the contents of this notice are
    A. train operator and superintendent
    B. signal maintainer and superintendent
    C. tower operator and train operator
    D. signal maintainer and tower operator

18. A train operator should use a route request button when
    A. the signal indicates proceed on main line
    B. a call-on is displayed
    C. the signal indicates stop
    D. the signal indicates proceed on diverging route

19. The PROPER way to request a route is to
    A. press the button corresponding to the desired route
    B. press the button a number of times to correspond with the number of the route requested
    C. stop at the signal and blow four short blasts
    D. stop at the signal and telephone the tower

20. The train operator will know that their requested route has been registered in the tower if
    A. a light comes on over the route request buttons
    B. an acknowledging signal is sounded on the tower horn
    C. the light in the route request button goes dark
    D. the home signal continues to indicate stop

21. It is clear that route request buttons
    A. eliminate train delays due to signals at junctions
    B. keep the tower operator alert
    C. force train operators and tower operators to be more careful
    D. are a more accurate form of communication than the whistle

Questions 22-29.

DIRECTIONS: Each of Questions 22 through 29, inclusive, is based on the rule immediately preceding the question. Read the rule carefully before answering the question. Be sure to consider only the information given in the rule immediately preceding the question.

RULE: When a gang or group is going to work under flagging protection at a given location, the office of the Superintendent of Transportation of the division must be notified.

22. Such notification is logically required MAINLY so that
    A. train operators may be alerted
    B. trains may be taken out of service
    C. delays may be avoided
    D. passengers may be informed of possible inconvenience

RULE: The person in charge of the work to be performed shall select the flaggers for each assignment from the list of qualified flagmen established in accordance with instructions of the General Superintendent.

23. This rule CLEARLY implies that
    A. the person in charge of a job trains the flagman or flagmen
    B. nearly all jobs require more than one flagman
    C. there is a list of qualified flagmen available
    D. the work of flagging should be divided equally among the qualified men

RULE: When necessary to signal a train to stop, the employee given such signal must continue to do so until the train has been brought to a stop or the train operator of the train has acknowledged the signal by sounding two short blasts of the whistle.

24. The two short blasts of the whistle are an indication that the
    A. employee giving the stop signal should continue giving the signal
    B. train operator has seen and understood the signal
    C. employee giving the stop signal should step into the clear
    D. train operator has made a full service brake application

25. This rule could NOT apply to _____ signals.
    A. hand   B. flag   C. lantern   D. fixed

RULE: Before coupling cars, train operators must see that the brake is set up on section to which coupling is to be made.

26. The brake is set up to
    A. prevent moving coupled cars with angle cocks closed
    B. make sure that the air lines are properly charged
    C. avoid damage to the couplers
    D. prevent rolling of cars to which coupling is made

RULE: Accident reports, facts, and conditions connected with accidents, and names of witnesses are confidential information. Employees must not communicate either orally or in writing to any person with reference to accidents except to proper officials of the system or except, with knowledge of the Authority, to the proper authorities entitled to such information.

27. The MOST nearly correct statement based on this rule is that
    A. an employee witnessing an accident may give information to system officials only
    B. an employee witnessing an accident should not make any written notes on the accident
    C. the names of witnesses of accidents is confidential information
    D. all accident reports must be given either orally or in writing

28. The MOST probable reason for having this rule is to
    A. prevent lawsuits
    B. avoid conflicting testimony
    C. prevent unofficial statements from being accepted as official
    D. conceal facts which may be damaging

RULE: In foggy weather or at any time when the train operator's vision is obstructed by snow, rain, sleet, or smoke, etc., they must run the train so that they can stop within range of vision in order to ensure the safety of the train and passengers.

29. This rule means MOST NEARLY that
    A. the braking distance in snow or sleet storms is about equal to the train operator's range of vision
    B. an train operator's vision is obstructed by fog about as much as it is by smoke
    C. when a train operator's range of vision is reduced, it is generally restricted by fog, snow, rain, sleet, or smoke
    D. if a train operator's view ahead is obstructed, he should operate his train slowly

30. If the motors continue to take power after the train operator of a passenger train has returned the master controller to OFF, his FIRST action in bringing the train back under control should be to
    A. signal for a car inspector
    B. release the master controller handle
    C. open the control switch
    D. reverse the motors

31. If a speed of 15 miles per hour is exactly 22 feet per second, then the number of miles per hour corresponding to 30 feet per second is MOST NEARLY
    A. 10   B. 15   C. 20   D. 25

32. If a train operator makes a brake application and holds it without either increasing or graduating off until the train comes to a stop, the result is ALMOST sure to be
    A. tripping the overload relay   B. overrunning the stop
    C. a hard stop   D. a skid

33. On approaching a home signal indicating STOP in the subway, the train operator observes a white light being moved rapidly up and down alongside the signal. The train operator should
    A. reduce speed and pass the signal slowly
    B. resume speed and pass the signal normally
    C. stop immediately and telephone for orders
    D. stop at the signal and find out who is waving the light

34. An train operator operating in a yard hears one long blast of the tower whistle. He should
    A. stop his train and await orders or a two-blast horn signal from the tower indicating all clear
    B. increase his speed to clear the switch he is on
    C. slow down to the yard speed limit
    D. continue and be on the watch for the signal maintainer

35. The MOST important reason for coasting as much as possible consistent with keeping on schedule is that this practice reduces
    A. brake shoe wear
    B. contact shoe wear
    C. wheel maintenance
    D. power consumption

36. The normal voltage of the third rail in the subway is NEAREST to _____ volts.
    A. 250   B. 400   C. 600   D. 750

37. A train operator operating their train in customer service approaches a home signal displaying three yellow (amber) lights. The train operator should
    A. stop their train and acknowledge the three yellow (amber) signals with a single horn blast before proceeding at reduced speed and extreme caution
    B. stop their train and contact the rail control center and question this line-up before moving
    C. proceed at a reduced speed using extreme caution expecting to find track personnel on or near the tracks
    D. proceed at normal speed but then reduce speed as they approach the next station expecting to find track personnel on or near the tracks

38. A and C Line trains operating on their normal route utilize which tunnel (tube) into and out of Manhattan?
    A. Montague Street tube
    B. Clark Street tube
    C. York Street tube
    D. Cranberry Street tube

39. A train operator operating their train in customer service was instructed by the rail control center to turn off their air ventilation system because of an odor of smoke. After doing so, this train operator should
    A. make an announcement apologizing for temporarily having to turn off the air ventilation
    B. say nothing to the customers and turn the air ventilation system back on when it is safe to do so
    C. make an announcement that you were instructed to turn off the air ventilation system because of an odor of smoke ahead
    D. say nothing to the customers and turn the air ventilation system on when the rail control center gives you permission

40. Part of a conductor's essential daily equipment is NOT which of the following? 40.____
    A. Rulebook
    B. Badge
    C. Drum switch key
    D. Safety vest

KEY (CORRECT ANSWERS)

1. D	11. B	21. D	31. C
2. B	12. D	22. A	32. C
3. B	13. B	23. C	33. D
4. A	14. C	24. B	34. A
5. D	15. D	25. D	35. D
6. D	16. A	26. D	36. C
7. B	17. C	27. C	37. B
8. C	18. C	28. C	38. D
9. B	19. A	29. D	39. B
10. C	20. A	30. C	40. C

TEST 3

DIRECTIONS: Each question or incomplete statement is followed by several suggested answers or completions. Select the one that BEST answers the question or completes the statement. *PRINT THE LETTER OF THE CORRECT ANSWER IN THE SPACE AT THE RIGHT.*

1. The PROPER way to move a car having inoperative air brakes from a lay-up track into the shop is to operate it slowly
    A. coupled to a car or cars with good brakes
    B. with a slight hand brake applied
    C. using the reverser to stop the car
    D. with a flagman walking ahead

   1.____

2. A train operator in the subway observes a white light moving up and down rapidly some distance ahead of their moving train. If their train has not passed any other warning lantern, the train operator should acknowledge the light with a whistle signal and
    A. stop
    B. reduce speed to 10 MPH
    C. proceed
    D. prepare to stop within range of vision

   2.____

3. Two positions of the master controller which are running positions are
    A. off and switching
    B. switching and series
    C. switching and multiple
    D. series and multiple

   3.____

4. Battery power is used on subway cars to supply energy to the
    A. car heaters
    B. fans
    C. main car lights
    D. emergency lights

   4.____

5. The dead-man feature on subway cars is inoperative whenever the
    A. controller is in the OFF position
    B. brake handle is in the release position
    C. reverser key is centered
    D. reverser key is reversed

   5.____

6. Train operators become acquainted with new regulations MAINLY through
    A. talking to other train operators
    B. school-car instruction
    C. notices posted on bulletin boards
    D. re-issues of the book of rules

   6.____

7. If an ambulance is required because someone is injured in the subway, train operators are instructed to notify the transit police department and have the transit police call for the ambulance. It is MOST important for the train operators to tell the transit police
   A. where the ambulance is needed
   B. his own name and badge number
   C. whether the injured party is male or female
   D. how severe the injuries are

Questions 8-20.

DIRECTIONS: Questions 8 through 20, inclusive, are based on the accompanying illustrations of color-light signals, signs, and markers used on the transit system. Since two schemes of signal indication and several forms of sign are in use on the transit system, a pair of illustrations having similar meanings are shown when necessary. In the accompanying illustrations, C O denotes that letters C and O are illuminated, S denotes an illuminated S sign, and (W) denotes auxiliary white lens illuminated.

8. The indication of this signal is
   A. stop and stay
   B. stop and then proceed, prepared to stop within vision
   C. proceed with caution at allowable speed
   D. proceed

9. This signal indicates
   A. stop and stay
   B. stop and then proceed, prepared to stop within vision
   C. proceed with caution at allowable speed
   D. proceed with caution

10. The indication of this signal is
    A. proceed with caution
    B. stop and then proceed, prepared to stop within vision
    C. proceed with caution at allowable speed
    D. proceed

11. This signal means
    A. proceed with caution
    B. stop and then proceed, prepared to stop within vision
    C. proceed expecting to find track occupied

11._____

12. The non-illuminated sign shown means
    A. cut-in power
    B. cut-out lights
    C. car stop
    D. coast

12._____

13. The non-illuminated sign shown is the
    A. station stop marker for 8-car trains
    B. turning point marker for 8-car trains
    C. beginning of coasting marker for 8-car trains
    D. marker for the point at which a 8-car train may resume normal speed

13._____

14. This sign is the
    A. station stop marker for 8-car trains
    B. turning point marker for 8-car trains
    C. beginning of coasting marker for 8-car trains
    D. marker for the point at which an 8-car train may resume normal speed

14._____

15. This illuminated sign is the
    A. station stop marker for 8-car trains
    B. turning point marker for 8-car trains
    C. beginning of coasting marker for 8-car trains
    D. marker for the point at which an 8-car train may resume normal speed

15._____

16. This sign means that
    A. there are no speed restrictions beyond this point
    B. signals beyond this point do not apply to trains
    C. train operators may operate without regard to rules beyond this point
    D. block signaling ends at this point

16._____

17. This signal aspect means switch set for _____ route pass expecting next signal to be _____.
    A. diverging; red
    B. straight; red
    C. diverging; green
    D. straight; green

17.____

18. This signal indicates proceed with caution
    A. into yard
    B. on diverging route
    C. on main route
    D. onto occupied track

18.____

19. The indication shown is
    A. proceed
    B. proceed on diverging route
    C. proceed on main route
    D. proceed with caution

19.____

20. The indication shown would MOST probably permit a train operator to
    A. operate the stop release and then proceed, prepared to stop within vision
    B. operate hand-throw switch and then proceed with caution
    C. enter inspection shed with caution
    D. proceed with caution onto yard lead

21. This signal aspect means that a train operator may
    A. proceed normally on either route
    B. pass expecting to find next signal on main route yellow or green
    C. proceed on diverging route
    D. proceed at not exceeding 25 MPH on main route

22. This signal indicates
    A. stop and blow whistle for route
    B. stop, operate stop release, then proceed with caution prepared to stop within range of vision
    C. stop and stay until a less restrictive aspect appears
    D. stop and telephone for orders

23. The aspect shown means
    A. stop and blow whistle for route
    B. stop, operate stop release, then proceed with caution, prepared to stop within range of vision
    C. stop and stay until a less restrictive aspect appears
    D. stop and telephone for orders

24. The indication of this illuminated sign is
    A. beginning of time control at indicated speed
    B. speed restricted to 15 MPH on curve
    C. take crossover at 15 MPH
    D. beginning of terminal track; maintain indicated speed

25. Three short whistle blasts are sounded to
    A. acknowledge a hand signal from someone on the track
    B. warn persons on or near the track to stand clear
    C. call for a transit police officer to meet the train
    D. ask for a car inspector to meet the train

26. If a subway train goes dead while it is running between stations, the train operator could conclude that the third rail was dead if the
    A. emergency lights in the train were dark
    B. main car lights were dark
    C. train operator's indication light went out
    D. tunnel lights were dark

27. Normally, when an express train is routed to the local tracks, the train operator is required to stop at
    A. certain specified busy stations only
    B. alternate stations
    C. express stations only
    D. all stations

28. Any signal imperfectly displayed is to be regarded as the most restrictive indication that can be given by that signal. Accordingly, the indication of an automatic signal which has both the green and yellow lenses illuminated is
    A. proceed with caution
    B. stop and then proceed according to rules
    C. stop and stay and contact the rail control center
    D. proceed with caution at allowable speed

29. A train operator observing the signal of Question 22 above is required by the rules to notify the
    A. superintendent of transportation   B. rail control center
    C. supervisor of signals   D. signal maintainer

30. The train operator of a train stopped in a station notices that there is considerable arcing underneath the car. His BEST initial action is to
    A. whistle for assistance   B. open the main knife switch
    C. contact the rail control center   D. open the control switch

31. The car stop markers for 4-, 5-, 6-, 7-, and 8-car trains at a certain station are located so that a properly stopped train of any length will be centered in the station. The distance between the 5-car and the 8-car stop markers MUST be _____ car lengths.
    A. 3   B. 2½   C. 2   D. 1½

32. Before starting the train to enter a shop building, the train operator MUST
    A. make a brake test   B. set out a warning flag or lantern
    C. sound the proper whistle signal   D. energize the shop third rail

33. A train operator is MOST likely to become aware of a grounded shoe beam on the operating car through the
    A. arcing and acrid odor
    B. tripping of the overload breaker
    C. loss of third rail power
    D. emergency application of the brakes

34. If there is a loss of third rail power and the train operator has permitted the train to coast to a stop between stations, he need NOT necessarily
    A. apply hand brakes   B. leave his cab
    C. telephone the rail control center   D. discharge passengers

35. When coupling cars on a grade, safety requires that the cars moved in making the coupling MUST be
    A. the longer section   B. moved upgrade
    C. the shorter section   D. moved downgrade

36. In making a report of an unusual occurrence on a train in the subway, the LEAST important information to include is
    A. time of day   B. weather
    C. head car number   D. direction of travel

8 (#3)

37. Entering a yard lay-up track, the train operator observes a red lantern on the rear of a car at the bumper. His BEST procedure is to
    A. sound his whistle and stop about a foot away
    B. stop a car length away and check with the workers
    C. couple to the car and apply brakes in emergency
    D. stop as soon as he sees the lantern and radio the dispatcher

38. Switch targets or pot signals are used in connection with switches that are operated
    A. pneumatically
    B. electrically
    C. hydraulically
    D. manually

39. Before moving a train in a yard, it is MOST important to check the
    A. brakes
    B. marker lights
    C. couplers
    D. battery

40. One person permitted to ride in the operating cab with the train operator is the
    A. conductor
    B. dispatcher
    C. tower operator
    D. superintendent

KEY (CORRECT ANSWERS)

1.	A	11.	A	21.	B	31.	D
2.	C	12.	D	22.	C	32.	C
3.	D	13.	A	23.	B	33.	A
4.	D	14.	B	24.	A	34.	D
5.	C	15.	D	25.	D	35.	B
6.	C	16.	D	26.	B	36.	B
7.	A	17.	A	27.	C	37.	B
8.	B	18.	C	28.	C	38.	D
9.	C	19.	B	29.	B	39.	A
10.	D	20.	D	30.	C	40.	D

TEST 4

DIRECTIONS: Each question or incomplete statement is followed by several suggested answers or completions. Select the one that BEST answers the question or completes the statement. *PRINT THE LETTER OF THE CORRECT ANSWER IN THE SPACE AT THE RIGHT.*

1. In a recent statement by the Transit Authority, their announced surplus was credited MOSTLY to
   A. more riders
   B. reductions in operating personnel
   C. sale of the power houses
   D. new cars and buses

   1.____

2. All train crews must have knowledge of the running time and are also required to know the scheduled time due at principal points and terminals. The MOST logical reason for this requirement is to make
   A. it possible for train crews to be contacted at any time
   B. both the train operator and the conductor responsible for having the train on time at these points
   C. certain that trains never leave principal points later than scheduled
   D. sure that the train crew is able to answer passengers' questions regarding time

   2.____

3. An operating rule states that, when a train is delayed in excess of four minutes for any cause whatsoever, either the train operator or the conductor shall contact the superintendent as soon as possible. The BEST reason for this procedure is so that the
   A. broadcasting companies can be notified of delays in train service
   B. blame for the delay can be properly placed
   C. rail control center can take immediate action
   D. train crew can find out the probable duration of the delay

   3.____

4. Train operators generally know the points at which coasting should be used under normal conditions by
   A. judgment gained through experience
   B. signal indications
   C. signs along the route
   D. bulletins posted at their home terminals

   4.____

5. A *call-on* signal is used only in conjunction with a(n) _____ signal.
   A. automatic   B. dwarf   C. approach   D. home

   5.____

135

6. Train crews shall be at their operating positions at least two minutes before the schedule time of departure of the train from the terminal. One possible reason for this requirement is that
   A. the train may be dispatched ahead of time in an emergency
   B. a substitute can be assigned in case of no-show
   C. the crew can discuss new bulletin orders
   D. the dispatcher can complete the entry on the sign-on sheet

7. Third rail power is used to operate the
   A. conductor's signal light
   B. car ventilating fans
   C. train operator's indication light
   D. tail lights

8. The time interval between trains is known as the
   A. gap
   B. layover time
   C. running time
   D. headway

9. A proceed hand signal may NEVER be given with a
   A. white light
   B. green lantern
   C. yellow lantern
   D. red lantern

10. A resume speed signal is a fixed signal located at a point where a train of
    A. any length may resume normal speed after a slow speed move
    B. indicated length, stopped to clear proper switches and signals for a reverse move, may proceed
    C. any length, which is operating in a time-controlled section, may proceed at normal speed
    D. indicated length, which has been running at reduced speed, may resume normal speed

11. At a blue light location in the subway, you would NOT ordinarily expect to find an emergency
    A. alarm box
    B. telephone
    C. fire extinguisher
    D. exit

12. Of the following, the one which is NOT a fixed signal is a
    A. coasting sign
    B. yellow lantern hung on a column
    C. slow sign
    D. bumper post light

13. A color-light signal which is never clear but always displays a red light is a _____ signal.
    A. home
    B. grade time
    C. curve
    D. dwarf marker

14. When an operator blows three short blasts on the train whistle, he is
    A. signaling for a transit police officer
    B. warning passengers standing too close to the platform edge
    C. calling for the car inspector
    D. acknowledging a lantern signal

15. According to rules, a subway train may move over a crossover for which no speed limiting sign is displayed at a MAXIMUM speed of _____ MPH.
    A. 8　　　B. 10　　　C. 12　　　D. 15

    15.____

16. One function of the emergency alarm system in the subway is to
    A. remove power from the third rail
    B. supply power to the car emergency lights
    C. provide a means of communication in the event of a power failure
    D. sound a warning in the nearest transit police office

    16.____

Questions 17-20.

DIRECTIONS:　Questions 17 through 20, inclusive, are based on the rule immediately preceding each question. Be sure to consider only the information given in the rule for each question.

RULE: Accident reports, facts, and conditions connected with accidents and names of witnesses are confidential information. Employees must not communicate either orally or in writing to any person with reference to accidents except to proper officials of the system or except, with knowledge of the Authority, to anyone entitled to such information.

17. The MOST likely reason for this rule is to
    A. avoid conflicting testimony
    B. prevent lawsuits
    C. conceal facts which may be damaging
    D. prevent unofficial statements from being accepted as official

    17.____

RULE: When operating a light train on the main line, train operators must never enter a station until they can get the entire train beyond the station.

18. According to this rule, a train operator operating a light train held out of a local station by an entering automatic signal which is red, may start to enter the station when he sees that the
    A. entering automatic signal has changed to yellow
    B. station area is clear of the train ahead
    C. leaving automatic signal has changed to yellow
    D. train in the station has started to move

    18.____

RULE: Employees required to work on or adjacent to tracks in the subway must not begin work on the track in any way without first displaying signal lights as follows:
Two lighted yellow lanterns approximately 500 feet in advance of the point of work;
A lighted red lantern not less than 75 feet in advance of the work;
A lighted green lantern at a safe distance beyond the work.

19. In this rule, a safe distance means MOST likely that the green lantern should be placed
    A. a train length past the yellow lights
    B. 75 feet past the red light
    C. a train length past workers on the track
    D. 500 feet past the yellow lights

RULE: Operators must not run ahead of schedule time unless ordered to do so by proper authority.

20. The MOST likely reason for this rule is based on the fact that trains running ahead of schedule
    A. have to be held at time points to get them back on schedule
    B. use more power as they do less coasting
    C. cause the train following to become overloaded and delayed
    D. disrupts the routine of employees working on tracks between train intervals

21. If an train operator receives a poorly executed hand or lantern signal so that they are not positive of the meaning, the BEST action for them to follow would be to
    A. assume the most likely meaning
    B. proceed cautiously
    C. stop immediately
    D. disregard the signal entirely

22. Of the following actions of a train operator, the one which would NOT be considered a violation of the rules would be to
    A. come to work without his watch
    B. stop his train in a station a car length beyond the car stop marker
    C. operate in regular passenger service with his cab door open
    D. sound several blasts of the whistle when skipping a regular passenger station

23. The rules state that, on straight yard track, the MAXIMUM speed at which the train may be operated is
    A. series   B. switching   C. multiple   D. 20 MPH

24. The PROPER speed at which cars should be brought together when coupling is nearest to _____ feet per _____.
    A. 2; second   B. 10; second   C. 2; minute   D. 10; minute

25. If in doubt as to the meaning of any rule, regulation, or instruction, the BEST procedure for a train operator to follow is to
    A. ask another train operator for an explanation
    B. obtain an explanation from the dispatcher
    C. use his own best judgment when a situation arises
    D. discuss the matter with his conductor

26. Sometimes conductors in passenger service close train doors without properly observing passengers entering or leaving the train. This is an improper action CHIEFLY because
    A. the conductor might strike a passenger with a closing door
    B. an exiting passenger might be left on the train
    C. passengers who hold doors open cannot be seen
    D. a passenger might be left on the platform

27. The protection of the *dead-man* feature on a moving train is lost when the
    A. train is coasting   B. brakes are applied in emergency
    C. reverser is centered   D. electric brake is not cut in

28. Single-track operation is generally necessary when
    A. a train with locked brakes blocks a main line
    B. signal cables are being replaced in an under-river tunnel
    C. running rails are being renewed in an express station
    D. lightbulbs are being replaced in an under-river tunnel

29. Unless the braking pressure is gradually reduced as the train nears a stop, the result will MOST likely be
    A. a hard stop   B. over-running the stop
    C. constant deceleration   D. a danger of skidding

30. A rule of the Transit Authority is that any employee must give his name and badge number when requested by a passenger
    A. only if a valid reason is given
    B. without delay or argument
    C. only if the passenger is insistent
    D. without argument, but only after first trying to placate the passenger

31. The law requires that subway cars in passenger service during the winter season must be kept heated between 40 and 65 degrees. It is MOST likely that these particular limits were picked because they
    A. result in minimum fogging of windows
    B. are the most comfortable year-round temperatures
    C. are most economical
    D. are comfortable for passengers wearing outdoor clothing

32. The LEAST valuable source for improvements in operating procedures is the
    A. suggestions of employees
    B. working agreement
    C. letters from passengers
    D. dispatcher's records

33. A six-track lay-up yard can hold twelve cars on each track, but there are already four ten-car trains in this yard. The number of additional cars that can be stored in this yard is
    A. 12	B. 32	C. 40	D. 72

34. A train operator, operating in a yard, hearing one long blast on the tower whistle, knows that the tower operator is signaling for
    A. all trains in the yard to come to an immediate stop
    B. the dispatcher to come to the tower
    C. a train on the yard leads to enter the yard
    D. the signal maintainer to call his field office

35. A train operator shows up to work smelling of alcohol but has NOT yet signed on to work. The FIRST duty of the supervisor is to
    A. send this employee to the transit clinic for substance abuse testing
    B. allow this employee to sign on the payroll and then immediately send them for substance abuse testing
    C. contact the area superintendent and the rail control center
    D. send the employee home immediately

KEY (CORRECT ANSWERS)

1.	A	11.	D	21.	C	31.	D
2.	B	12.	B	22.	D	32.	B
3.	C	13.	D	23.	A	33.	B
4.	C	14.	C	24.	A	34.	A
5.	D	15.	B	25.	B	35.	C
6.	A	16.	A	26.	A		
7.	B	17.	D	27.	C		
8.	D	18.	C	28.	B		
9.	D	19.	C	29.	A		
10.	D	20.	C	30.	B		

TEST 5

DIRECTIONS: Each question or incomplete statement is followed by several suggested answers or completions. Select the one that BEST answers the question or completes the statement. *PRINT THE LETTER OF THE CORRECT ANSWER IN THE SPACE AT THE RIGHT.*

1. Train operators' reporting times are usually 10 to 15 minutes before their trains are scheduled to depart. Of the following, the LEAST important reason for this time interval is to allow the train operator to
   A. change into his working clothes
   B. check the condition of his train
   C. check that his conductor has signed in
   D. take care of any personal needs

2. A train operator taking a lay-up train over the road to a yard
   A. must operate from a standing position
   B. may not exceed 10 MPH at any time
   C. may follow the train ahead of him as close as safety permits
   D. must observe certain special rules

3. The position to which the master controller handle has been moved by the train operator determines the
   A. braking power available
   B. availability of the *dead-man*'s feature
   C. maximum speed to which the train may accelerate

4. When a train operator's indication light is illuminated, it is an indication that
   A. all brakes are released
   B. the third rail is alive
   C. all side doors are closed and locked
   D. the main car fuse is okay

5. The type of signal used at congested stations to *close-in* trains is known as a _____ signal.
   A. repeater
   B. station time
   C. grade time
   D. train order

6. It is generally true that the principal cause of MOST accidents is
   A. fatigue
   B. physical disability
   C. carelessness
   D. sabotage

7. The BEST way for a train operator to acquaint themselves with new regulations as soon as possible is to
   A. study the book of rules
   B. depend on specific notice by the train service supervisor
   C. be alert to the needs of the service
   D. read all bulletins as issued

8. Loss of third rail power on a subway car will FIRST prevent functioning of the
   A. air compressor
   B. train whistle
   C. service brakes
   D. pneumatically operated doors

9. Timetables are often made up so that both local and express trains are scheduled to arrive at a station at the same time in order to afford passengers an opportunity to change trains. From the passengers' viewpoint, it is MOST important for timetables to be so made up when the
   A. headways are short
   B. express stations are far apart
   C. local and express trains are bound for different terminals
   D. headways are long

10. Train operators are required to coast as much as possible consistent with running on time. The MOST important reason for coasting is that it reduces
    A. wheel maintenance
    B. brake shoe wear
    C. power consumption
    D. contact shoe arcing

11. A facing point switch is a switch the points of which
    A. face in the direction of traffic flow
    B. make up against the face of rail
    C. face approaching traffic
    D. face the tower

12. Trains of two converging routes approach a junction at the same time. It is logical to assume that the train which should go FIRST is the one which
    A. does arrive first
    B. is carrying the greater passenger load
    C. has the greater number of cars
    D. is scheduled to arrive first

13. If the running time between the two towers at the ends of a certain tunnel is 3½ minutes, the MINIMUM headway in one direction when single-tracking is operated is _____ minutes.
    A. 3½   B. 7   C. 10½   D. 14

14. A train operator should be particularly alert to guard against sliding the wheels on a yard track
    A. when the rails have been renewed
    B. during a long dry spell
    C. at the beginning of a light rain
    D. immediately after the rails have been polished

15. The purpose of a contact shoe slipper is to
    A. simplify the removal of a badly worn contact shoe
    B. insulate the contact shoe from the third rail
    C. make the shoe slid easily on the third rail
    D. ensure good contact with the third rail

16. A train operator, operating a train in regular service, observes three lighted yellow lanterns displayed alongside of his track. The train operator should
    A. slow down and sound one long and one short whistle blast
    B. slow down and sound two short whistle blasts
    C. proceed normally
    D. stop for instructions from the first flagman

17. Opening the trip cock on a subway car will ordinarily result in
    A. an emergency brake application
    B. the electric brake becoming inoperative
    C. a service brake application
    D. releasing the brakes

18. When a train operator is reporting a fire by phone, it would be LEAST important for them to report
    A. the time when he noticed the fire
    B. the location of the fire
    C. his name and pass number
    D. the nature of the trouble

19. When the train operator of a passenger train descends to the track to the track to check his train because the brakes fail to release, he need NOT
    A. take the reverser key with him
    B. set up a hand brake
    C. inform the conductor
    D. pull the emergency alarm

20. During the time when 15 trains pass a certain point on one track in one hour, the headway on that track, in minutes, is
    A. 2   B. 4   C. 8   D. 15

21. An express train requires five minutes to make the run between two stations which are two miles apart. The average speed of the train, in miles per hour, for this run is
    A. 20   B. 24   C. 30   D. 36

22. Hand brakes are to be set up on three cars of a ten-car train laid up on a grade. If the cars are numbered 1 to 10 starting with the car that is highest on the grade, it would be BEST to set up the hand brakes on
    A. cars 1, 2, and 3
    B. cars 2, 5, and 9
    C. cars 8, 9, and 10
    D. any three cars

23. After applying the required number of hand brakes on a train which has been laid up on a grade, the PROPER test of whether the hand brakes will hold the train is to
    A. examine each hand brake chain to see that it is right
    B. apply the brakes in emergency
    C. place the brake valve in release
    D. apply one point of power to see if the train will move

24. The term *automatic stop*, as used on the transit system, means a   24.____
    A. device used by a conductor to apply the brakes in emergency
    B. device on the roadway which applies the brakes when a train passes a red signal
    C. scheduled stop for an express operating on the local track
    D. train stop which is initiated by the train operator

25. Unused sections of track should be operated over at more or less regular intervals to make sure that   25.____
    A. any rust on the rails will be worn off
    B. the roadbed is being properly maintained
    C. no obstructions have been placed in the path of a train
    D. the switches are in good operating condition

26. A train operator, operating a train in regular service, sees an individual step out of the way of the train and wave a green lantern up and down. The train operator should   26.____
    A. sound two short whistle blasts and proceed normally
    B. sound a succession of short whistle blasts and proceed normally
    C. stop for identification of the individual
    D. proceed normally with no whistle response

27. If a transit employee saw a passenger knocked down on the station platform by another passenger who was rushing to the train, the FIRST action to be taken by the employee should be to   27.____
    A. ascertain if the passenger was injured
    B. get the names of witnesses
    C. report the incident to the transit police
    D. obtain the passengers' names and addresses

28. Three green lightbulbs at a terminal positioned nearest the conductor's position when illuminated tell the conductor to   28.____
    A. keep train doors open for a connection with an arriving train
    B. close down doors and notify the train operator to proceed
    C. secure train and report to the dispatcher's office
    D. make all local stops

29. A repeater signal is MOST usually found on   29.____
    A. elevated structures   B. curves
    C. yards   D. leaving terminals

30. The three MAIN radio frequencies used by subway personnel are   30.____
    A. B1, B2, and C1   B. A division, B1, and B2
    C. A1, A2, and B division   D. 101, 102, and 103

KEY (CORRECT ANSWERS)

1.	C	11.	C	21.	B
2.	D	12.	D	22.	C
3.	C	13.	B	23.	C
4.	C	14.	C	24.	B
5.	B	15.	B	25.	A
6.	C	16.	B	26.	A
7.	D	17.	A	27.	A
8.	A	18.	A	28.	B
9.	D	19.	D	29.	B
10.	C	20.	B	30.	B

READING COMPREHENSION
UNDERSTANDING AND INTERPRETING WRITTEN MATERIAL
EXAMINATION SECTION
TEST 1

DIRECTIONS: Each question or incomplete statement is followed by several suggested answers or completions. Select the one that BEST answers the question or completes the statement. *PRINT THE LETTER OF THE CORRECT ANSWER IN THE SPACE AT THE RIGHT.*

Questions 1-8.

DIRECTIONS: Questions 1 through 8 are to be answered on the basis of the following regulations governing Newspaper Carriers when on subway trains or station platforms. These Newspaper Carriers are issued badges which entitle them to enter subway stations, when carrying papers in accordance with these regulations, without paying a fare.

REGULATIONS GOVERNING NEWSPAPER CARRIERS WHEN ON SUBWAY TRAINS OR STATION PLATFORMS

1. Carriers must wear badges at all times when on trains.
2. Carriers must not sort, separate, or wrap bundles on trains or insert sections.
3. Carriers must not obstruct platform of cars or stations.
4. Carriers may make delivery to stands inside the stations by depositing their badge with the station agent.
5. Throwing of bundles is strictly prohibited and will be cause for arrest.
6. Each bundle must not be over 18" x 12" x 15".
7. Not more than two bundles shall be carried by each carrier. (An extra fare to be charged for a second bundle.)
8. No wire to be used on bundles carried into stations.

1. These regulations do NOT prohibit carriers on trains from _____ newspapers.

   A. sorting bundles of
   B. carrying bundles of
   C. wrapping bundles of
   D. inserting sections into

2. A carrier delivering newspapers to a stand inside of the station MUST

   A. wear his badge at all times
   B. leave his badge with the railroad clerk
   C. show his badge to the railroad clerk
   D. show his badge at the newsstand

3. Carriers are warned against throwing bundles of newspapers from trains MAINLY because these acts may

   A. wreck the stand
   B. cause injury to passengers
   C. hurt the carrier
   D. damage the newspaper

4. It is permissible for a carrier to temporarily leave his bundles of newspapers 4.____

   A. near the subway car's door
   B. at the foot of the station stairs
   C. in front of the exit gate
   D. on a station bench

5. Of the following, the carrier who should NOT be restricted from entering the subway is 5.____
   the one carrying a bundle which is _____ long, _____ wide, and _____ high.

   A. 15"; 18"; 18"   B. 18"; 12"; 18"
   C. 18"; 12"; 15"   D. 18"; 15"; 15"

6. A carrier who will have to pay one fare is carrying _____ bundle(s). 6.____

   A. one   B. two   C. three   D. four

7. Wire may NOT be used for tying bundles because it may be 7.____

   A. rusty
   B. expensive
   C. needed for other purposes
   D. dangerous to other passengers

8. If a carrier is arrested in violation of these regulations, the PROBABLE reason is that he 8.____

   A. carried too many papers
   B. was not wearing his badge
   C. separated bundles of newspapers on the train
   D. tossed a bundle of newspapers to a carrier on a train

Questions 9-12.

DIRECTIONS: Questions 9 through 12 are to be answered on the basis of the Bulletin printed below. Read this Bulletin carefully before answering these questions. Select your answers ONLY on the basis of this Bulletin.

BULLETIN

Rule 107(m) states, in part, that *Before closing doors they (Conductors) must afford passengers an opportunity to detrain and entrain...*

Doors must be left open long enough to allow passengers to enter and exit from the train. Closing doors on passengers too quickly does not help to shorten the station stop and is a violation of the safety and courtesy which must be accorded to all our passengers.

The proper and effective way to keep passengers moving in and out of the train is to use the public address system. When the train is excessively crowded and passengers on the platform are pushing those in the cars, it may be necessary to close the doors after a reasonable period of time has been allowed.

Closing doors on passengers too quickly is a violation of rules and will be cause for disciplinary actions.

9. Which of the following statements is CORRECT about closing doors on passengers too quickly? It

   A. will shorten the running time from terminal to terminal
   B. shortens the station stop but is a violation of safety and courtesy
   C. does not help shorten the station stop time
   D. makes the passengers detrain and entrain quicker

10. The BEST way to get passengers to move in and out of cars quickly is to

    A. have the platform conductors urge passengers to move into doorways
    B. make announcements over the public address system
    C. start closing doors while passengers are getting on
    D. set a fixed time for stopping at each station

11. The conductor should leave doors open at each station stop long enough for passengers to

    A. squeeze into an excessively crowded train
    B. get from the local to the express train
    C. get off and get on the train
    D. hear the announcements over the public address system

12. Closing doors on passengers too quickly is a violation of rules and is cause for

    A. the conductor's immediate suspension
    B. the conductor to be sent back to the terminal for another assignment
    C. removal of the conductor at the next station
    D. disciplinary action to be taken against the conductor

Questions 13-15.

DIRECTIONS: Questions 13 through 15 are to be answered on the basis of the Bulletin printed below. Read this Bulletin carefully before answering these questions. Select your answers ONLY on the basis of this Bulletin.

BULLETIN

Conductors assigned to train service are not required to wear uniform caps from June 1 to September 30, inclusive.

Conductors assigned to platform duty are required to wear the uniform cap at all times. Conductors are reminded that they must furnish their badge numbers to anyone who requests same.

During the above-mentioned period, conductors may remove their uniform coats. The regulation summer short-sleeved shirts must be worn with the regulation uniform trousers. Suspenders are not permitted if the uniform coat is removed. Shoes are to be black but sandals, sneakers, suede, canvas, or two-tone footwear must not be worn.

Conductors may work without uniform tie if the uniform coat is removed. However, only the top collar button may be opened. The tie may not be removed if the uniform coat is worn.

13. Conductors assigned to platform duty are required to wear uniform caps

    A. at all times except from June 1 to September 30, inclusive
    B. whenever they are on duty
    C. only from June 1 to September 30, inclusive
    D. only when they remove their uniform coats

14. Suspenders are permitted ONLY if conductors wear

    A. summer short-sleeved shirts with uniform trousers
    B. uniform trousers without belt loops
    C. the type permitted by the authority
    D. uniform coats

15. A conductor MUST furnish his badge number to

    A. authority supervisors only
    B. members of special inspection only
    C. anyone who asks him for it
    D. passengers only

Questions 16-17.

DIRECTIONS: Questions 16 and 17 are to be answered SOLELY on the basis of the following Bulletin.

BULLETIN

Effective immediately, Conductors on trains equipped with public address systems shall make the following announcements in addition to their regular station announcement. At stations where passengers normally board trains from their homes or places of employment, the announcement shall be *Good Morning* or *Good Afternoon* or *Good Evening,* depending on the time of the day. At stations where passengers normally leave trains for their homes or places of employment, the announcement shall be *Have a Good Day* or *Good Night,* depending on the time of day or night.

16. The MAIN purpose of making the additional announcements mentioned in the Bulletin is MOST likely to

    A. keep passengers informed about the time of day
    B. determine whether the public address system works in case of an emergency
    C. make the passengers' ride more pleasant
    D. have the conductor get used to using the public address system

17. According to this Bulletin, a conductor should greet passengers boarding the *D* train at the Coney Island Station at 8 A.M. Monday by announcing

    A. Have a Good Day
    B. Good Morning
    C. Watch your step as you leave
    D. Good Evening

Questions 18-25.

DIRECTIONS: Questions 18 through 25 are to be answered on the basis of the information regarding the incident given below. Read this information carefully before answering these questions.

INCIDENT

As John Brown, a cleaner, was sweeping the subway station platform, in accordance with his assigned schedule, he was accused by Henry Adams of unnecessarily bumping him with the broom and scolded for doing this work when so many passengers were on the platform. Adams obtained Brown's badge number and stated that he would report the matter to the Transit Authority. Standing around and watching this were Mary Smith, a schoolteacher, Ann Jones, a student, and Joe Black, a maintainer, with Jim Roe, his helper, who had been working on one of the turnstiles. Brown thereupon proceeded to take the names and addresses of these people as required by the Transit Authority rule which directs that names and addresses of as many disinterested witnesses be taken as possible. Shortly thereafter, a train arrived at the station and Adams, as well as several other people, boarded the train and left. Brown went back to his work of sweeping the station.

18. The cleaner was sweeping the station at this time because

   A. the platform was unusually dirty
   B. there were very few passengers on the platform
   C. he had no regard for the passengers
   D. it was set by his work schedule

19. This incident proves that

   A. witnesses are needed in such cases
   B. porters are generally careless
   C. subway employees stick together
   D. brooms are dangerous in the subway

20. Joe Black was a

   A. helper   B. maintainer
   C. cleaner   D. teacher

21. The number of persons witnessing this incident was

   A. 2   B. 3   C. 4   D. 5

22. The addresses of witnesses are required so that they may later be

   A. depended on to testify   B. recognized
   C. paid   D. located

23. The person who said he would report this incident to the transit authority was

   A. Black   B. Adams   C. Brown   D. Roe

24. The ONLY person of the following who positively did NOT board the train was

    A. Brown B. Smith C. Adams D. Jones

25. As a result of this incident,

    A. no action need be taken against the cleaner unless Adams makes a written complaint
    B. the cleaner should be given the rest of the day off
    C. the handles of the brooms used should be made shorter
    D. Brown's badge number should be changed

KEY (CORRECT ANSWERS)

1. B
2. B
3. B
4. D
5. C

6. A
7. D
8. D
9. C
10. B

11. C
12. D
13. B
14. D
15. C

16. C
17. B
18. D
19. A
20. B

21. C
22. D
23. B
24. A
25. A

TEST 2

DIRECTIONS: Each question or incomplete statement is followed by several suggested answers or completions. Select the one that BEST answers the question or completes the statement. *PRINT THE LETTER OF THE CORRECT ANSWER IN THE SPACE AT THE RIGHT.*

Questions 1-10.

DIRECTIONS: Questions 1 through 10 are to be answered on the basis of the information contained in the following safety rules. Read the rules carefully before answering these questions.

SAFETY RULES

Employees must take every precaution to prevent accidents, or injury to persons, or damage to property. For this reason, they must observe conditions of the equipment and tools with which they work, and the structures upon which they work.

It is the duty of all employees to report to their superior all dangerous conditions which they may observe. Employees must use every precaution to prevent the origin of fire. If they discover smoke or a fire in the subway, they shall proceed to the nearest telephone and notify the trainmaster giving their name, badge number, and location of the trouble.

In case of accidents on the subway system, employees must, if possible, secure the name, address, and telephone number of any passengers who may have been injured.

Employees at or near the location of trouble on the subway system, whether it be a fire or an accident, shall render all practical assistance which they are qualified to perform.

1. The BEST way for employees to prevent an accident is to

   A. secure the names of the injured persons
   B. arrive promptly at the location of the accident
   C. give their name and badge numbers to the trainmaster
   D. take all necessary precautions

2. In case of trouble, trackmen are NOT expected to

   A. report fires
   B. give help if they don't know how
   C. secure telephone numbers of persons injured in subway accidents
   D. give their badge number to anyone

3. Trackmen MUST

   A. be present at all fires
   B. see all accidents
   C. report dangerous conditions
   D. be the first to discover smoke in the subway

4. Observing conditions means to

   A. look at things carefully
   B. report what you see
   C. ignore things that are none of your business
   D. correct dangerous conditions

5. A dangerous condition existing on the subway system which a trackman should observe and report to his superior would be

   A. passengers crowding into trains
   B. trains running behind schedule
   C. tools in defective condition
   D. some newspapers on the track

6. If a trackman discovers a badly worn rail, he should

   A. not take any action
   B. remove the worn section of rail
   C. notify his superior
   D. replace the rail

7. The MAIN reason a trackman should observe the condition of his tools is

   A. so that they won't be stolen
   B. because they don't belong to him
   C. to prevent accidents
   D. because they cannot be replaced

8. If a passenger who paid his fare is injured in a subway accident, it is MOST important that an employee obtain the passenger's

   A. name
   B. age
   C. badge number
   D. destination

9. An employee who happens to be at the scene of an accident on a crowded station of the system should

   A. not give assistance unless he chooses to do so
   B. leave the scene immediately
   C. question all bystanders
   D. render whatever assistance he can

10. If a trackman discovers a fire at one end of a station platform and telephones the information to the trainmaster, he need NOT give

    A. the trainmaster's name
    B. the name of the station involved
    C. his own name
    D. the number of his badge

Questions 11-15.

DIRECTIONS: Questions 11 through 15 are to be answered on the basis of the information contained in the safety regulations given below. Refer to these rules in answering these questions.

REGULATIONS FOR SMALL GROUPS WHO MOVE FROM POINT TO POINT ON THE TRACKS

Employees who perform duties on the tracks in small groups and who move from point to point along the trainway must be on the alert at all times and prepared to clear the track when a train approaches without unnecessarily slowing it down. Underground at all times, and out-of-doors between sunset and sunrise, such employees must not enter upon the tracks unless each of them is equipped with an approved light. Flashlights must not be used for protection by such groups. Upon clearing the track to permit a train to pass, each member of the group must give a proceed signal, by hand or light, to the motorman of the train. Whenever such small groups are working in an area protected by caution lights or flags, but are not members of the gang for whom the flagging protection was established, they must not give proceed signals to motormen. The purpose of this rule is to avoid a motorman's confusing such signal with that of the flagman who is protecting a gang. Whenever a small group is engaged in work of an engrossing nature or at any time when the view of approaching trains is limited by reason of curves or otherwise, one man of the group, equipped with a whistle, must be assigned properly to warn and protect the man or men at work and must not perform any other duties while so assigned.

11. If a small group of men are traveling along the tracks toward their work location and a train approaches, they should

    A. stop the train
    B. signal the motorman to go slowly
    C. clear the track
    D. stop immediately

12. Small groups may enter upon the tracks

    A. only between sunset and sunrise
    B. provided each has an approved light
    C. provided their foreman has a good flashlight
    D. provided each man has an approved flashlight

13. After a small group has cleared the tracks in an area unprotected by caution lights or flags,

    A. each member must give the proceed signal to the motorman
    B. the foreman signals the motorman to proceed
    C. the motorman can proceed provided he goes slowly
    D. the last member off the tracks gives the signal to the motorman

14. If a small group is working in an area protected by the signals of a track gang, the members of the small group

    A. need not be concerned with train movement
    B. must give the proceed signal together with the track gang

C. can delegate one of their members to give the proceed signal
D. must not give the proceed signal

15. If the view of approaching trains is blocked, the small group should

    A. move to where they can see the trains
    B. delegate one of the group to warn and protect them
    C. keep their ears alert for approaching trains
    D. refuse to work at such locations

Questions 16-25.

DIRECTIONS: Questions 16 through 25 are to be answered SOLELY on the basis of the article about general safety precautions given below.

GENERAL SAFETY PRECAUTIONS

When work is being done on or next to a track on which regular trains are running, special signals must be displayed as called for in the general rules for flagging. Yellow caution signals, green clear signals, and a flagman with a red danger signal are required for the protection of traffic and workmen in accordance with the standard flagging rules. The flagman shall also carry a white signal for display to the motorman when he may proceed. The foreman in charge must see that proper signals are displayed.

On elevated lines during daylight hours, the yellow signal shall be a yellow flag, the red signal shall be a red flag, the green signal shall be a green flag, and the white signal shall be a white flag. In subway sections, and on elevated lines after dark, the yellow signal shall be a yellow lantern, the red signal shall be a red lantern, the green signal shall be a green lantern, and the white signal shall be a white lantern.

Caution and clear signals are to be secured to the elevated or subway structure with non-metallic fastenings outside the clearance line of the train and on the motorman's side of the track.

16. On elevated lines during daylight hours, the caution signal is a

    A. yellow lantern   B. green lantern
    C. yellow flag   D. green flag

17. In subway sections, the clear signal is a

    A. yellow lantern   B. green lantern
    C. yellow flag   D. green flag

18. The MINIMUM number of lanterns that a subway track flagman should carry is

    A. 1   B. 2   C. 3   D. 4

19. The PRIMARY purpose of flagging is to protect the

    A. flagman   B. motorman
    C. track workers   D. railroad

20. A suitable fastening for securing caution lights to the elevated or subway structure is   20.____

    A. copper nails   B. steel wire
    C. brass rods   D. cotton twine

21. On elevated structures during daylight hours, the red flag is held by the   21.____

    A. motorman   B. foreman   C. trackman   D. flagman

22. The signal used in the subway to notify a motorman to proceed is a   22.____

    A. white lantern   B. green lantern
    C. red flag   D. yellow flag

23. The caution, clear, and danger signals are displayed for the information of   23.____

    A. trackmen   B. workmen   C. flagmen   D. motormen

24. Since the motorman's cab is on the right-hand side, caution signals should be secured to the   24.____

    A. right-hand running rail
    B. left-hand running rail
    C. structure to the right of the track
    D. structure to the left of the track

25. In a track work gang, the person responsible for the proper display of signals is the   25.____

    A. track worker   B. foreman
    C. motorman   D. flagman

KEY (CORRECT ANSWERS)

1.	D	11.	C
2.	B	12.	B
3.	C	13.	A
4.	A	14.	D
5.	C	15.	B
6.	C	16.	C
7.	C	17.	B
8.	A	18.	B
9.	D	19.	C
10.	A	20.	D

21. D
22. A
23. D
24. C
25. B

TEST 3

DIRECTIONS: Each question or incomplete statement is followed by several suggested answers or completions. Select the one that BEST answers the question or completes the statement. *PRINT THE LETTER OF THE CORRECT ANSWER IN THE SPACE AT THE RIGHT.*

Questions 1-6.

DIRECTIONS: Questions 1 through 6 are to be answered on the basis of the Bulletin Order given below. Refer to this bulletin when answering these questions.

BULLETIN ORDER NO. 67

SUBJECT: Procedure for Handling Fire Occurrences

In order that the Fire Department may be notified of all fires, even those that have been extinguished by our own employees, any employee having knowledge of a fire must notify the Station Department Office immediately on telephone extensions D-4177, D-4181, D-4185, or D-4189.

Specific information regarding the fire should include the location of the fire, the approximate distance north or south of the nearest station, and the track designation, line, and division.

In addition, the report should contain information as to the status of the fire and whether our forces have extinguished it or if Fire Department equipment is required.

When all information has been obtained, the Station Supervisor in Charge in the Station Department Office will notify the Desk Trainmaster of the Division involved.

Richard Roe,
Superintendent

1. An employee having knowledge of a fire should FIRST notify the

   A. Station Department Office
   B. Fire Department
   C. Desk Trainmaster
   D. Station Supervisor

1.____

2. If bulletin order number 1 was issued on January 2, bulletins are being issued at the monthly average of

   A. 8   B. 10   C. 12   D. 14

2.____

3. It is clear from the bulletin that

   A. employees are expected to be expert fire fighters
   B. many fires occur on the transit system
   C. train service is usually suspended whenever a fire occurs
   D. some fires are extinguished without the help of the Fire Department

3.____

4. From the information furnished in this bulletin, it can be assumed that the

   A. Station Department office handles a considerable number of telephone calls
   B. Superintendent Investigates the handling of all subway fires
   C. Fire Department is notified only in ease of large fires
   D. employee first having knowledge of the fire must call all 4 extensions

5. The PROBABLE reason for notifying the Fire Department even when the fire has been extinguished by a subway employee is because the Fire Department is

   A. a city agency
   B. still responsible to check the fire
   C. concerned with fire prevention
   D. required to clean up after the fire

6. Information about the fire NOT specifically required is

   A. track   B. time of day   C. station   D. division

Questions 7-10.

DIRECTIONS: Questions 7 through 10 are to be answered on the basis of the paragraph on fire fighting shown below. When answering these questions, refer to this paragraph.

FIRE FIGHTING

A security officer should remember the cardinal rule that water or soda acid fire extinguishers should not be used on any electrical fire, and apply it in the case of a fire near the third rail. In addition, security officers should familiarize themselves with all available fire alarms and fire-fighting equipment within their assigned posts. Use of the fire alarm should bring responding Fire Department apparatus quickly to the scene. Familiarity with the fire-fighting equipment near his post would help in putting out incipient fires. Any man calling for the Fire Department should remain outside so that he can direct the Fire Department to the fire. As soon as possible thereafter, the special inspection desk must be notified, and a complete written report of the fire, no matter how small, must be submitted to this office. The security officer must give the exact time and place it started, who discovered it, how it was extinguished, the damage done, cause of same, list of any injured persons with the extent of their injuries, and the name of the Fire Chief in charge. All defects noticed by the security officer concerning the fire alarm or any fire-fighting equipment must be reported to the special inspection department.

7. It would be PROPER to use water to put out a fire in a(n)

   A. electric motor   B. electric switch box
   C. waste paper trash can   D. electric generator

8. After calling the Fire Department from a street box to report a fire, the security officer should then

   A. return to the fire and help put it out
   B. stay outside and direct the Fire Department to the fire
   C. find a phone and call his boss
   D. write out a report for the special inspection desk

9. A security officer is required to submit a complete written report of a fire   9._____

   A. two weeks after the fire
   B. the day following the fire
   C. as soon as possible
   D. at his convenience

10. In his report of a fire, it is NOT necessary for the security officer to state   10._____

    A. time and place of the fire
    B. who discovered the fire
    C. the names of persons injured
    D. quantity of Fire Department equipment used

Questions 11-16.

DIRECTIONS: Questions 11 through 16 are to be answered on the basis of the Notice given below. Refer to this Notice in answering these questions.

NOTICE

Your attention is called to Route Request Buttons that are installed on all new type Interlocking Home Signals where there is a choice of route in the midtown area. The route request button is to be operated by the motorman when the home signal is at danger and no call-on is displayed or when improper route is displayed.

To operate, the motorman will press the button for the desiredroute as indicated under each button; a light will then go on over the buttons to inform the motorman that his request has been registered in the tower.

If the towerman desires to give the motorman a route other than the one he selected, the towerman will cancel out the light over the route selection buttons. The motorman will then accept the route given.

If no route or call-on is given, the motorman will sound his whistle for the signal maintainer, secure his train, and call the desk trainmaster.

11. The official titles of the two classes of employee whose actions would MOST frequently be affected by the contents of this notice are   11._____

    A. motorman and trainmaster
    B. signal maintainer and trainmaster
    C. towerman and motorman
    D. signal maintainer and towerman

12. A motorman should use a route request button when   12._____

    A. the signal indicates proceed on main line
    B. a call-on is displayed
    C. the signal indicates stop
    D. the signal indicates proceed on diverging route

13. The PROPER way to request a route is to 13.____

    A. press the button corresponding to the desired route
    B. press the button a number of times to correspond with the number of the route requested
    C. stop at the signal and blow four short blasts
    D. stop at the signal and telephone the tower

14. The motorman will know that his requested route has been registered in the tower if 14.____

    A. a light comes on over the route request buttons
    B. an acknowledging signal is sounded on the tower horn
    C. the light in the route request button goes dark
    D. the home signal continues to indicate stop

15. Under certain conditions, when stopped at such home signal, the motorman must signal for a signal maintainer and call the desk trainmaster. 15.____
    Such condition exists when, after standing awhile,

    A. the towerman continues to give the wrong route
    B. the towerman does not acknowledge the signal
    C. no route or call-on is given
    D. the light over the route request buttons is cancelled out

16. It is clear that route request buttons 16.____

    A. eliminate train delays due to signals at junctions
    B. keep the towerman alert
    C. force motormen and towermen to be more careful
    D. are a more accurate form of communication than the whistle.

Questions 17-22.

DIRECTIONS: Questions 17 through 22 are to be answered on the basis of the instructions for removal of paper given below. Read these instructions carefully before answering these questions.

GENERAL INSTRUCTIONS FOR REMOVAL OF PAPER

When a cleaner's work schedule calls for the bagging of paper, he will remove paper from the waste paper receptacles, bag it, and place the bags at the head end of the platform, where they will be picked up by the work train. He will fill bags with paper to a weight that can be carried without danger of personal injury, as porters are forbidden to drag bags of paper over the platform. Cleaners are responsible that all bags of paper are arranged so as to prevent their falling from the platform to tracks, and so as to not interfere with passenger traffic.

17. A GOOD reason for removing the paper from receptacles and placing it in bags is that bags are more easily 17.____

    A. stored   B. weighed   C. handled   D. emptied

18. The *head end* of a local station platform is the end 18._____

    A. in the direction that trains are running
    B. nearest to which the trains stop
    C. where there is an underpass to the other side
    D. at which the change booth is located

19. The MOST likely reason for having the filled bags placed at the head end of the station rather than at the other end is that 19._____

    A. a special storage space is provided there for them
    B. this end of the platform is farthest from the passengers
    C. most porters' closets are located near the head end
    D. the work train stops at this end to pick them up

20. Limiting the weight to which the bags can be filled is PROBABLY done to 20._____

    A. avoid having too many ripped or broken bags
    B. protect the porter against possible rupture
    C. make sure that all bags are filled fairly evenly
    D. insure that, when stored, the bags will not fall to the track

21. The MOST important reason for not allowing filled bags to be dragged over the platform is that the bags 21._____

    A. could otherwise be loaded too heavily
    B. might leave streaks on the platform
    C. would wear out too quickly
    D. might spill paper on the platform

22. The instructions do NOT hold a porter responsible for a bag of paper which 22._____

    A. is torn due to dragging over a platform
    B. falls on a passenger because it was poorly stacked
    C. falls to the track without being pushed
    D. is ripped open by school children

Questions 23-25.

DIRECTIONS: Questions 23 through 25 are to be answered on the basis of the situation described below. Consider the facts given in this situation when answering these questions.

SITUATION

A new detergent that is to be added to water and the resulting mixture just wiped on any surface has been tested by the station department and appeared to be excellent. However, you notice, after inspecting a large number of stations that your porters have cleaned with this detergent, that the surfaces cleaned are not as clean as they formerly were when the old method was used.

23. The MAIN reason for the station department testing the new detergent in the first place was to make certain that 23._____

    A. it was very simple to use
    B. a little bit would go a long way
    C. there was no stronger detergent on the market
    D. it was superior to anything formerly used

24. The MAIN reason that such a poor cleaning job resulted was MOST likely due to the 24._____

    A. porters being lax on the job
    B. detergent not being as good as expected
    C. incorrect amount of water being mixed with the detergent
    D. fact that the surfaces cleaned needed to be scrubbed

25. The reason for inspecting a number of stations was to 25._____

    A. determine whether all porters did the same job
    B. insure that the result of the cleaning job was the same in each location
    C. be certain that the detergent was used in each station inspected
    D. see whether certain surfaces cleaned better than others

---

KEY (CORRECT ANSWERS)

1.	A	11.	C
2.	C	12.	C
3.	D	13.	A
4.	A	14.	A
5.	C	15.	C
6.	B	16.	D
7.	C	17.	C
8.	B	18.	A
9.	C	19.	D
10.	D	20.	B

21. C
22. D
23. D
24. B
25. B

READING COMPREHENSION
UNDERSTANDING AND INTERPRETING WRITTEN MATERIAL
EXAMINATION SECTION
TEST 1

DIRECTIONS: Each question or incomplete statement is followed by several suggested answers or completions. Select the one that BEST answers the question or completes the statement. *PRINT THE LETTER OF THE CORRECT ANSWER IN THE SPACE AT THE RIGHT.*

Questions 1-6.

DIRECTIONS: Questions 1 through 6, inclusive, are based SOLELY on the information contained in the following paragraphs.

MODEL XXX BUS AIR SUSPENSION SYSTEM

The bus air suspension system is made up of suspension supports, air bellows, height control valves, radius rods, and shock absorbers. The supports provide the means by which the suspension system is connected to the axles. The system operates automatically and maintains a constant ride height regardless of load or of load distribution.

Vertical loads are supported by eight rubberized nylon air bellows assemblies. Four bellows are used at the front axle, and four double convolution bellows are used at the rear axle. Bellows are installed between beams in the coach body structure and suspension supports attached to axles. The bellows upper bead is clamped between the lower retainer and the piston. When the bellows assembly is installed, the beads form air-tight seals. The rear (double convolution) bellows form seals on the adapter plates which are mounted on the suspension support and upper mounting plate.

The air pressure in the air bellows is varied automatically in proportion to the vehicle load by height control valves. Three height control valves, one at the front axle and two at the rear axle, maintain constant vehicle ride height for all load conditions. The height control valve levers are connected to the axles by links.

The front control valve has a single supply outlet connected to a *tee* in the delivery line to the bellows on both sides.

Radius rods, four at each axle, transmit driving and braking forces from the axles to the coach body. These rods also control the lateral and longitudinal position of each axle under the vehicle. Each end of the radius rod contains a rubber bushing that requires no lubrication. Telescoping type, double-acting shock absorbers are mounted at the ends of each axle. The stabilizer bar, attached in rubber mountings to the body, is linked at both ends to the rear suspension supports.

1. According to the above paragraph, the ride height　　　　　　　　　　　　　　　　1._____

   A. varies in proportion to the vehicle load
   B. varies in proportion to bus speed
   C. is constant for all load conditions
   D. varies in proportion to the braking forces

2. The use of double convolution bellows is limited to _____ axle(s).　　　　　　2._____

   A. the right front　　　　　　B. both front
   C. the right rear　　　　　　　D. both rear

3. The lower retainer is a component which forms a part of the　　　　　　　　　　3._____

   A. coach body structure　　　B. bellows clamp
   C. bellows piston　　　　　　　D. bellows upper bead

4. Air is supplied to the front bellows on both sides through a　　　　　　　　　　4._____

   A. tee　　　　B. piston　　　　C. link　　　　D. lever

5. The position of the axles under the vehicle is controlled by the　　　　　　　　5._____

   A. air bellows　　　　　　　　B. height control valves
   C. radius rods　　　　　　　　D. shock absorbers

6. The stabilizer bar is　　　　　　　　　　　　　　　　　　　　　　　　　　　　　　　6._____

   A. a double-acting type
   B. a telescoping type
   C. installed between beams in the body
   D. linked to the rear suspension supports

Questions 7-12.

DIRECTIONS: Questions 7 through 12, inclusive, are based on the Information for Operators given below. Read this information carefully before answering these items.

INFORMATION FOR OPERATORS

In spite of caution signs and signal lights, more than 42% of all automobile accidents occur at intersections. In narrow city streets with narrow sidewalks and heavy traffic, you should approach intersections at 15 miles per hour with your foot just touching the brake pedal; in wet weather 10 miles per hour. At rural intersections, be sure you have a clear view of the intersecting road to the right and left at least 300 feet before you reach the intersection, otherwise slow down.

At an intersection, the vehicle on your right has the right-of-way if both of you reach the intersection at the same time. You have the right-of-way over the vehicle at your left under the same condition, but must not insist upon it if there is risk of a collision.

Do not pass another vehicle at an intersection. Stop your vehicle to allow pedestrians to cross in front of you at intersections if they have stepped off the curb. Operators must use extreme caution when approaching or turning at intersections not controlled by a signal light.

7. One of the facts given is that 7.____

   A. nearly all accidents occur at country crossroads
   B. nearly half of all accidents occur at traffic lights in cities
   C. approximately two-fifths of all accidents occur where roads or streets cross one another
   D. 42% of all accidents occur on narrow city streets

8. According to this information, if you are approaching an intersection at which there is no traffic light, and a man has started to cross the street in front of you, you must 8.____

   A. reduce your speed to 15 miles per hour
   B. blow your horn lightly
   C. stop to allow him to cross
   D. place your foot so it just touches the brake pedal

9. At an intersection not protected by a traffic light, you should grant the right-of-way to the vehicle approaching from the 9.____

   A. right if it is 300 feet from the intersection
   B. left if it is 300 feet from the intersection
   C. opposite direction if its right turn indicator is flashing
   D. left or the right if there is danger of a collision

10. In the information, it is clearly stated that an intersection should be approached at 15 miles per hour if you 10.____

    A. are driving on a narrow city street in heavy traffic
    B. do not see a warning sign 300 feet from the intersection
    C. do not intend to pass the vehicle ahead
    D. see a car stopped on the intersecting street waiting to cross

11. The information clearly states that 11.____

    A. most city streets are narrow
    B. all city intersections should be approached at 10 miles per hour
    C. passing another vehicle at an intersection is forbidden
    D. there is a clear view of rural intersections from a distance of 300 feet

12. The type of accident referred to probably does NOT include the striking of a 12.____

    A. pedestrian by a railroad train
    B. pedestrian by a passenger car
    C. bus by a taxicab
    D. bus by a truck

Questions 13-21.

DIRECTIONS: Questions 13 through 21, inclusive, are based on the Bus Operator Instructions given below. Read these instructions carefully before answering these questions.

BUS OPERATOR INSTRUCTIONS

When running on public streets, operators must have all running lights on during hours of darkness. Practices such as having bus interior lights burning during daylight hours or operating after dark with only half the interior lights burning are forbidden. Tampering with the light circuits and removing fuses therefrom is forbidden. Poor driving practices such as sudden starts and stops, striking curbs, spinning wheels, sliding wheels, riding with hand brake half on, or operating the bus with badly overheated or knocking engine must be avoided. Tires must be frequently inspected to detect improper inflation. When adjusting inside or outside rear view mirrors, the use of force is prohibited, since only mild pressure is required. If adjustment cannot be made by use of mild pressure, report the assembly as defective.

13. Bus operators are forbidden to

    A. inspect tires
    B. remove light fuses
    C. adjust viewing mirrors
    D. stop close to curb

14. The MOST important reason for NOT operating a bus with the engine knocking is to prevent

    A. the noise
    B. loss of power
    C. waste of gas
    D. engine damage

15. A bus operator is required to make a report with respect to

    A. sliding wheels
    B. striking curbs
    C. spinning wheels
    D. stuck mirrors

16. Running lights on a bus operating on city streets would be required before 6 P.M. on every day in the month of

    A. December   B. April   C. June   D. August

17. All interior bus lights should be on when the bus

    A. is garaged for the night
    B. is being repaired
    C. is operating on public streets after dark
    D. fuses are all in place

18. Operating during daylight hours with bus interior lights on is forbidden in order to avoid

    A. a traffic violation
    B. passenger complaints
    C. unsafe bus operation
    D. unnecessary battery drain

19. Riding with the hand brake half on

    A. is a good safety practice
    B. is sometimes permissible
    C. does not cause brake wear
    D. is forbidden

20. The bus operator is required to

    A. repair tires
    B. repair defective mirror assemblies
    C. inspect tires
    D. make sudden starts

21. Making frequent sudden stops would be LEAST likely to cause

    A. improper tire inflation
    B. excessive brake wear
    C. passenger discomfort
    D. rear end collisions

Questions 22-25.

DIRECTIONS: Questions 22 through 25, inclusive, are based on the regulations relating to voting on Primary Day as given below. Read these regulations carefully before answering these questions.

REGULATIONS RELATING TO VOTING ON PRIMARY DAY

The polls are open from 3:00 to 10:00 P.M. Employees who are on duty Primary Day during the period polls are open, and who would not have two consecutive hours free time to vote, will be granted leave of absence for two hours without loss of pay.

Examples:
1. Employees reporting for work at 3 P.M. to and including 4:59 P.M. will be allowed two hours leave with pay.
2. Employees who report to work at 5 P.M. or thereafter, no time to be allowed.
3. Employees who complete their tour of duty and are cleared on or before 8 P.M., no time to be allowed.

22. A two-hour leave of absence with pay will be granted to employees who are on duty Primary Day if they

    A. have to work two hours while the polls are open
    B. would not have two consecutive hours free time to vote
    C. are working a day tour
    D. are working a night tour

23. An employee working an evening tour will be allowed two hours with pay if he has to report for work at _____ P.M.

    A. 3:00   B. 5:00   C. 7:00   D. 9:00

24. An employee working an afternoon tour will be allowed two hours with pay if he clears at _____ P.M.

    A. 6:00   B. 7:00   C. 8:00   D. 9:00

25. An employee working an afternoon tour will NOT be allowed any time off if he clears at _____ P.M.

    A. 8:00   B. 8:30   C. 9:30   D. 10:00

KEY (CORRECT ANSWERS)

1. C
2. D
3. B
4. A
5. C

6. D
7. C
8. C
9. D
10. A

11. C
12. A
13. B
14. D
15. D

16. A
17. C
18. D
19. D
20. C

21. A
22. B
23. A
24. D
25. A

TEST 2

DIRECTIONS: Each question or incomplete statement is followed by several suggested answers or completions. Select the one that BEST answers the question or completes the statement. *PRINT THE LETTER OF THE CORRECT ANSWER IN THE SPACE AT THE RIGHT.*

Questions 1-8.

DIRECTIONS: Questions 1 through 8 are to be answered on the basis of the information contained in the trackmen duties given below. Read these duties carefully before answering these questions.

TRACKMEN DUTIES

Trackmen will report to and receive orders from assistant foremen of track. Trackmen will install, inspect, repair, replace, and maintain tracks, ties, ballast, track rail fastenings, and track rail electrical insulating joints. Additional duties of trackmen include clearing of tracks in case of accidents, snow removal and tamping of ballast. Further duties of trackmen include such work in train storage yards or on road tracks, within the qualifications of their position, as their superiors may direct.

1. Trackmen receive their orders

    A. only from a foreman of track
    B. from either an assistant foreman or a foreman of track
    C. only from an assistant foreman of track
    D. from any foreman

2. A PROBABLE reason for assigning trackmen to snow removal is because

    A. trackmen cannot do their regular work when it snows
    B. snow removal is heavy work
    C. trackmen can make any necessary repairs at the same time
    D. tracks in yards and on elevated lines must be cleared of snow

3. Inspection of track rails is

    A. performed only by foremen
    B. only done after accidents
    C. the only inspection work performed by a trackman
    D. only one important duty of the trackman

4. A trackman's duties on trackwork do NOT include

    A. replacing track
    B. installing ties
    C. installing insulated joints
    D. repairing station platforms

1.____

2.____

3.____

4.____

5. The duties statement shows that trackmen MUST

   A. do any assigned work in connection with track
   B. often act as supervisors
   C. be able to do any work in the subway
   D. do other work when there is no trackwork

6. Tamping is a job USUALLY done in connection with

   A. inspection of insulated joints
   B. ballast work
   C. repair of rail fastenings
   D. snow removal

7. The rail fastenings which trackmen repair are for the

   A. third rail
   B. track rails
   C. turnstile railings
   D. station platform railings

8. The track rail insulated joints are designed to provide _____ insulation.

   A. electrical   B. heat   C. sound   D. vibration

Questions 9-17.

DIRECTIONS: Questions 9 through 17 are to be answered on the basis of the information contained in the Instructions on Trackwork given below. Read these rules carefully before answering these questions.

INSTRUCTIONS ON TRACKWORK

Tie plates shall be used under rails on all ties except at insulated joints. Bolts through insulating bushings are not to be driven through, but inserted by hand. Guard rails are to be bolted to running rails with standard bolts, using spring washers, head locks, and flat washers. Rail braces shall be spiked with screw spikes. When removing or reinserting screw spikes, care must be taken not to destroy the thread in the wood tie. If a cut spike (nail type) is withdrawn for any reason, the hole is to be filled with a square creosoted plug and the spike re-driven in the same location. Ties are to be pulled by hand. No picks, shovels, or spike mauls are to be used for pulling ties.

9. Ties should be pulled

   A. with spike mauls
   B. with shovels
   C. by hand
   D. with picks

10. Tie plates are used

    A. on all ties
    B. only at insulated joints
    C. except at insulated joints
    D. on alternate ties

11. Rail braces shall have

    A. insulators
    B. bolts
    C. cut spikes
    D. screw spikes

12. Plugs are to be   12.____

    A. square B. free of creosote
    C. round   D. driven by hand

13. Guard rails are fastened to running rails with   13.____

    A. special bolts B. standard bolts
    C. insulators   D. plugs

14. Bolts through insulating bushings are to be   14.____

    A. hand inserted B. non-standard
    C. elliptical   D. driven

15. When cut spikes are withdrawn from a tie, the hole is to be   15.____

    A. insulated B. rethreaded
    C. left open D. plugged

16. Head locks and spring washers are used on   16.____

    A. guard rail bolts B. screw spikes
    C. tie plates   D. cut spikes

17. Screw spike holes in a tie   17.____

    A. may be reused
    B. must be plugged with a round plug
    C. are not to be reused
    D. must always be rethreaded

Questions 18-25.

DIRECTIONS: Questions 18 through 25, inclusive, are to be answered on the basis of the description of the Subway Car Air Compressor System given below. Read this information carefully before answering these questions.

SUBWAY CAR AIR COMPRESSOR SYSTEM

A two-stage, motor-driven air compressor having a large low pressure cylinder and a smaller high pressure cylinder is used. The low pressure cylinder, fitted with an air intake filter, performs the first stage of compression and discharges through an intercooler into the high pressure cylinder where the second stage of compression is performed. An unloader valve insures that compression does not begin until the motor has reached its full speed. An aftercooler is located between the compressor discharge and a compressor reservoir. An automatic drain valve located on the compressor reservoir automatically discharges precipitated moisture from the reservoir whenever the compressor governor functions to cut in power or shut off power to the compressor motor. The governor operates to stop the compressor when the reservoir air pressure reaches 140 lbs. and to start the compressor when the reservoir air pressure drops to 125 lbs. A safety valve set at 150 lbs. is connected to the compressor reservoir.

18. The number of air cooling devices provided in the compressor system is

    A. 1   B. 2   C. 3   D. 4

19. When the motor is starting up, it is protected by the

    A. safety valve   B. governor
    C. drain valve   D. unloader valve

20. The intake filter is MOST likely designed to screen out

    A. dirt   B. water   C. oil   D. heat

21. The air pressure is LOWEST in the

    A. small cylinder   B. large cylinder
    C. compressor reservoir   D. aftercooler

22. The automatic drain valve is triggered by the

    A. governor   B. unloader valve
    C. safety valve   D. intercooler

23. The motor should stop running when the reservoir air pressure reaches _____ lbs.

    A. 125   B. 130   C. 135   D. 140

24. Water automatically drains from the

    A. low pressure cylinder   B. high pressure cylinder
    C. air reservoir   D. intercooler

25. Compression begins with the motor

    A. off   B. at low speed
    C. at intermediate speed D. at full speed

KEY (CORRECT ANSWERS)

1. B
2. D
3. D
4. D
5. A

6. B
7. B
8. A
9. C
10. C

11. D
12. A
13. B
14. A
15. D

16. A
17. A
18. B
19. D
20. A

21. B
22. A
23. D
24. C
25. D

TEST 3

DIRECTIONS: Each question or incomplete statement is followed by several suggested answers or completions. Select the one that BEST answers the question or completes the statement. *PRINT THE LETTER OF THE CORRECT ANSWER IN THE SPACE AT THE RIGHT.*

Questions 1-4.

DIRECTIONS: Questions 1 through 4 are to be answered on the basis of the following information.

<u>TRESPASSERS ON TRANSIT AUTHORITY SURFACE PROPERTIES</u>

Your attention is again directed to the need for rigid controls to prevent unauthorized persons from entering Transit Authority property.

All strangers or persons who are not recognized as having official business on the property will be questioned by the first member of supervision who encounters them and such persons will be ejected immediately upon failure to present authorization or valid reason for being on the property.

In all cases where trespassers refuse to leave the property, or offer physical resistance to ejection, the Transit Authority police will be promptly notified for assistance and all members of supervision present will assist in the immediate identification and ejection of the trespassers.

Where property protection employees are assigned, they too will be notified.

Immediately following the call for Transit police assistance, notice of the circumstances will be given to Surface Control on Extension B6-504.

All Surface Transportation employees must be advised that entrance and exit from Surface properties must be through authorized locations only, and failure to comply will be considered a flagrant disregard for outstanding regulations.

Finally, a complete written report is to be forwarded to the Assistant General Superintendent, Operations, of all instances dealing with the above:

1. The following are four possible cases that might be correct in which a supervisor may eject a person whom he does not recognize from Transit Authority property: The person
    I. has a legitimate reason for being on Transit Authority property
    II. presents authorization for being on Transit Authority property
    III. has accidently wandered onto Transit Authority property
    IV. has no proof of his identity
Which of the following choices lists ALL of the above cases that are CORRECT?

   A. I and II
   B. I and III
   C. II and IV
   D. III and IV

1._____

2. If a supervisor is uncertain that a person who he does not know has official business on Transit Authority property, the FIRST action that the supervisor should take is to

   A. eject the person
   B. call the Transit Authority police
   C. call other members of supervision for assistance
   D. question the person

3. When an unauthorized person has been ejected from Transit Authority property, a written report of the incident must be forwarded to

   A. the Superintendent of Operations
   B. Surface Control
   C. the Assistant General Superintendent, Operations
   D. the Location Chief

4. The following are four possible situations that might be CORRECT in which the Transit Authority Police should be notified for assistance:
   I. A trespasser refuses to leave Transit Authority property
   II. A trespasser is encountered on Transit Authority property
   III. A stranger enters Transit Authority property through an unauthorized entrance
   IV. A trespasser physically resists ejection

Questions 5-12.

DIRECTIONS: Questions 5 through 12 are to be answered on the basis of the information contained in the rules for reporting fires given below. Read the rules carefully before answering these questions.

RULES FOR REPORTING FIRES

If a fire occurs in the subway or in the cars, the person discovering same shall, except in the case of very small fires, go to the nearest telephone and notify the trainmaster. If a fire occurs on a bus, the person discovering same shall, except in the case of very small fires, go to the nearest telephone and notify the Central Dispatch Office. In both cases, the person making the call should give the location of the fire, his name, his badge number, and the department in which employed. In the case of a very small fire, the person discovering same shall use all means in his power to extinguish it promptly using fire extinguishers, sand pails, water buckets, or other equipment readily available. A complete report of the fire, including the location from which the extinguisher or other equipment was taken, should be transmitted promptly to the employee's department head.

5. A fire discovered in the subway should be reported to the

   A. fire department
   B. police department
   C. trainmaster
   D. Central Dispatch Office

6. A fire discovered on a bus should be reported to the

   A. fire department
   B. police department
   C. trainmaster
   D. Central Dispatch Office

7. The employee discovering a fire should report same by use of the NEAREST 7.____

   A. fire alarm box
   B. gong
   C. telephone
   D. messenger

8. A trackman on duty is LEAST likely to discover a fire 8.____

   A. in the subway
   B. on an elevated line
   C. on a bus
   D. in a train storage yard

9. The employee discovering a very small fire should 9.____

   A. notify the trainmaster immediately
   B. wait and see if it will spread before reporting it
   C. go for assistance to extinguish it
   D. try to put it out promptly

10. An employee's report on a very small fire would NOT include the 10.____

    A. cost to repair the damage
    B. name of the employee reporting
    C. location of the extinguisher used
    D. date on which the fire occurred

11. The employee's complete report of a fire must identify the extinguisher used MAINLY so that 11.____

    A. it will be refilled or replaced
    B. its effectiveness can be checked
    C. the location of the fire will be recorded
    D. its contents will not be wasted

12. For large fires, the complete report required in the last sentence of the above rules is a written report because 12.____

    A. a written report is most accurate
    B. the fire may involve a criminal offense
    C. the original report was made orally
    D. it provides a permanent record

Questions 13-22.

DIRECTIONS: Questions 13 through 22, inclusive, are to be answered on the basis ONLY of the Description of Porter's Equipment given below. Read this description carefully before answering these questions.

DESCRIPTION OF PORTER'S EQUIPMENT

The Tampico Brush has white hard bristles and is used to apply soap solution when cleaning columns and tile. The Palmyra Brush has very hard red bristles and is used to scrub gutters, booth floors, and urinal stands. The Milwaukee Push Broom is approximately 3 feet in length, with black semi-hard bristles and is used for sweeping floors. The Rinsing Brush has very soft bristles and is used to wash away all soap solution after surfaces have been scrubbed. The Fibre Broom has reddish-brown stiff fibres, and is used to sweep stairways. Utility Boxes, containing compartments for sawdust, sand, and salt, are located at the ends of station platforms.

13. Stairway steps are cleaned with the

    A. Push Broom B. Tampico Brush
    C. Palmyra Brush D. Fibre Broom

14. The Push Broom has a length of APPROXIMATELY _____ inches.

    A. 48   B. 36   C. 20   D. 18

15. Soap solution is applied to tile with a _____ brush.

    A. Palmyra B. soft-bristle
    C. red-bristle D. Tampico

16. The brush with very soft bristles is used for

    A. rinsing   B. sweeping   C. scrubbing   D. dusting

17. The material which is LEAST likely to be stored in a Utility Box is

    A. sand   B. salt   C. sawdust   D. soap

18. Columns are cleaned with the

    A. Fibre Broom B. Push Broom
    C. Tampico Brush D. Palmyra Brush

19. The Fibre Broom has fibres whose color is

    A. pure white B. solid red
    C. jet black D. reddish-brown

20. Sand is stored at the

    A. booths B. stairways
    C. exit gates D. platform ends

21. The MINIMUM number of compartments in the Utility Boxes must be

    A. 4   B. 3   C. 2   D. 1

22. Urinal stands are scrubbed with a

    A. Tampico Brush B. Push Broom
    C. Rinsing Brush D. Palmyra Brush

Questions 23-25.

DIRECTIONS: Questions 23 through 25 are to be answered SOLELY on the basis of the following Directive. Read this Directive carefully before answering the questions.

DIRECTIVE

When work trains having miscellaneous equipment (flat cars, crane cars, etc.) are in transit, the following flagging and safety instructions must be adhered to:

1. When flat cars are at the forward end of a train, the Flagman will station himself on the leading car. The Flagman will keep in constant communication with the Motorman through the use of sound-powered telephones. If sound-powered telephones become defective and alternate means of communications are needed, the Command Center must be called for instructions. Positive communications must be maintained while the train is in motion. Any loss of communication will be a signal for the Motorman to *Stop and Investigate*.

2. When flat cars are trailing, the Flagman will station himself on the rear of the last motor car in a position to view the trailing cars. Flagmen must observe that tail lights are illuminated at all times.

3. At all times when these trains are stopped for any reason, Motorman must sound two blasts of the whistle or horn before proceeding.

4. Safety demands that Motormen and Flagmen investigate all causes of a train going into emergency; particularly when an employee is known to be riding a flat car.

5. Under no circumstances will an employee walk across a flat car while a train is in motion.

23. When flat cars are at the forward end of a work train, the Flagman will station himself _____ car.

    A. at the rear of the last motor
    B. on the trailing flat
    C. on the leading flat
    D. at the front of the first motor

24. When a train with flat cars has stopped and the Motorman wishes to proceed again, he MUST

    A. call the Command Center
    B. shout instructions to the Flagman
    C. check that the Flagman is using the correct signals
    D. sound two blasts of the whistle or horn

25. When there is a loss of positive communication between the Motorman and the Flagman while the train is in motion, the Motorman should

    A. tell the Flagman to use his flashlight for flagging
    B. stop the train and investigate the situation
    C. tell the Flagman to use hand signals for flagging
    D. put the train into emergency

KEY (CORRECT ANSWERS)

1. D
2. D
3. C
4. B
5. C

6. D
7. C
8. C
9. D
10. A

11. A
12. D
13. D
14. B
15. D

16. A
17. D
18. C
19. D
20. D

21. B
22. D
23. C
24. D
25. B

READING COMPREHENSION
UNDERSTANDING AND INTERPRETING WRITTEN MATERIAL

EXAMINATION SECTION
TEST 1

DIRECTIONS: Each question or incomplete statement is followed by several suggested answers or completions. Select the one that BEST answers the question or completes the statement. *PRINT THE LETTER OF THE CORRECT ANSWER IN THE SPACE AT THE RIGHT.*

Questions 1-10.

DIRECTIONS: Questions 1 through 10 are to be answered on the basis of the description of an incident given below. Read the description carefully before answering these questions.

DESCRIPTION OF INCIDENT

On Tuesday, October 8, at about 4:00 P.M., bus operator Sam Bell, Badge No. 3871, whose accident record was perfect, was operating his half-filled bus, No. 4392Y, northbound and on schedule along Dean Street. At this time, a male passenger who was apparently intoxicated started to yell and to use loud and profane language. The bus driver told this passenger to be quiet or to get off the bus. The passenger said that he would not be quiet but indicated that he wanted to get off the bus by moving toward the front door exit. When he reached the front of the bus, which at the time was in motion, the intoxicated passenger slapped the bus operator on the back and pulled the steering wheel sharply. This action caused the bus to sideswipe a passenger automobile coming from the opposite direction before the operator could stop the bus. The sideswiped car was a red 2007 Pontiac 2-door convertible, License 6416-KN, driven by Albert Holt. The bus driver kept the doors of his bus closed and blew the horn vigorously. The horn blowing was quickly answered as Sergeant Henry Burns, Badge No. 1208, and Patrolman Joe Cross, Badge No. 24643, happened to be following a few cars behind the bus in police car No. 736. The intoxicated passenger, who gave his name as John Doe, was placed under arrest, and Patrolman Cross took the names of witnesses while Sergeant Burns recorded the necessary vehicular information. Investigation showed that no one was injured in the accident and that the entire damage to the automobile was having its side slightly pushed in.

1. From the information given, it can be reasoned that

    A. it was just beginning to rain
    B. Dean Street is a two-way street
    C. there were mostly women shoppers on the bus
    D. most seats in the bus were filled

2. The name of the policeman who was riding in the police car with the sergeant was

    A. Cross   B. Bell   C. Holt   D. Burns

2 (#1)

3. From the description, it is evident that the passenger automobile was traveling   3.____

   A. north   B. south   C. east   D. west

4. It is logical to conclude that the passenger automobile was damaged on its   4.____

   A. front end
   B. rear end
   C. right side
   D. left side

5. A fact concerning the intoxicated passenger that is clearly stated in the above description is that he   5.____

   A. was intoxicated when he got on the bus
   B. hit a fellow passenger
   C. pulled the steering wheel sharply
   D. was not arrested

6. The bus operator called the attention of the police by   6.____

   A. sideswiping an oncoming car
   B. yelling and using profane language
   C. blowing his horn vigorously
   D. stopping a police car coming from the opposite direction

7. A reasonable conclusion that can be drawn from the above description is that   7.____

   A. the name John Doe was fictitious
   B. the sideswiped automobile was from out of town
   C. some of the passengers on the bus were injured
   D. the bus operator tried to put the intoxicated passenger off the bus

8. The number of the police car involved in the incident was   8.____

   A. 4392Y   B. 6416-KN   C. 1208   D. 736

9. From the facts stated, it is obvious that the bus operator was   9.____

   A. behind schedule
   B. driving too close to the center of the street
   C. discourteous to the intoxicated passenger
   D. a good driver

10. It is clearly stated that the   10.____

    A. sideswiped automobile was a blue sedan
    B. bus driver kept the bus doors closed until the police came
    C. incident happened on a Thursday
    D. police sergeant took down the names of witnesses

Questions 11-20.

DIRECTIONS: Questions 11 through 20 are to be answered on the basis of the paragraph below covering cleaning supplies. Refer to this paragraph when answering these questions.

CLEANING SUPPLIES

Certain amounts of cleaning supplies are used each week at each station of the Transit Authority. The following information applies to a station of average size. For cleaning floors, tiles, and toilets, approximately 14 pounds of soap powder is used each week. A scouring powder is used to clean unusually difficult stains, and approximately 1 1/2 pounds is used in a week. A disinfectant solution is used for cleaning telephone alcoves, toilets, and booth floors, and approximately 1 quart of undiluted disinfectant is used each week. To make a regular strength disinfectant solution, 1/4 ounce of undiluted disinfectant is added to 14 gallons of water. One pint of lemon oil is used each week to polish metal surfaces in booths and in other station areas.

11. In a period of 4 weeks, the amount of soap powder that is used at the average station is MOST NEARLY _____ pounds.

    A. 48   B. 52   C. 56   D. 60

12. In a period of 1 year, the amount of scouring powder that is used at the average station is MOST NEARLY _____ pounds.

    A. 26   B. 52   C. 64   D. 78

13. If a certain large station uses 1 1/2 times the soap powder that an average station uses, then the larger station uses MOST NEARLY _____ pounds a week.

    A. 14   B. 21   C. 24   D. 28

14. To make a regular strength disinfectant solution, the number of ounces of undiluted disinfectant that should be added to 3 gallons of water is

    A. 4   B. 3/4   C. 1   D. 1 1/4

15. To make a double strength disinfectant solution, the number of ounces of undiluted disinfectant that should be added to 3 gallons of water is

    A. 4   B. 3/4   C. 1   D. 1 1/2

16. In a period of 4 weeks, the amount of lemon oil that is used at the average station is _____ gallon(s).

    A. 1/4   B. 4   C. 1   D. 1 1/2

17. In a period of one year, the amount of soap powder that is used at 5 average stations is MOST NEARLY _____ pounds.

    A. 260   B. 728   C. 3,640   D. 5,260

18. To clean a station that is difficult to remove, it would be BEST for a porter to use

    A. soap powder   B. scouring powder
    C. disinfectant solution D. lemon oil

19. Lemon oil should be used for

   A. scouring
   B. regular cleaning
   C. polishing metal surfaces
   D. disinfecting

20. If a smaller than average station uses 3/4 of the amount of scouring powder than an average station uses, then in one week the amount of scouring powder used at the smaller station is MOST NEARLY _____ pound(s).

   A. 7/8   B. 1   C. 1 1/8   D. 1 1/4

Questions 21-25.

DIRECTIONS: Questions 21 through 25, inclusive, are to be answered on the basis of the bus cleaning instructions below, which should be performed in the order given. Read the instructions carefully before answering these questions.

   1. SPRAY wheels and mud guards with hand water hose to remove loose dirt.
   2. SCRUB mud guards with brush and cleaner.
   3. SCRUB wheels with brush and cleaner.
   4. SCRAPE grease from wheels with hand scraper.
   5. RINSE wheels and mud guards with hand water hose.

21. The cleaning instructions which involve the same parts of the bus are

   A. 1 and 2   B. 1 and 3   C. 2 and 4   D. 1 and 5

22. The scraping takes place

   A. *after* both the spraying and rinsing
   B. *after* the rinsing but before the scrubbing
   C. *before* both the scrubbing and rinsing
   D. *before* the rinsing but after the spraying

23. The hand water hose is NOT used to remove the grease because water

   A. cannot remove the grease properly
   B. would injure the motor
   C. has to be used as cleaner solution
   D. is used only for spraying

24. The brush is used in connection with operations

   A. 1 and 2   B. 2 and 3   C. 3 and 4   D. 4 and 5

25. Loose dirt is removed by

   A. scraping   B. scrubbing   C. spraying   D. rinsing

KEY (CORRECT ANSWERS)

1. B
2. A
3. B
4. D
5. C

6. C
7. A
8. D
9. D
10. B

11. C
12. D
13. B
14. A
15. C

16. B
17. C
18. B
19. C
20. C

21. D
22. D
23. A
24. B
25. C

TEST 2

DIRECTIONS: Each question or incomplete statement is followed by several suggested answers or completions. Select the one that BEST answers the question or completes the statement. *PRINT THE LETTER OF THE CORRECT ANSWER IN THE SPACE AT THE RIGHT.*

Questions 1-8.

DIRECTIONS: Questions 1 through 8 are to be answered on the basis of the information contained in the safety rules given. Read these rules carefully before answering these questions.

SAFETY RULES FOR EMPLOYEES WORKING ON TRACKS

Always carry a hand lantern whenever walking a track and walk opposite to the direction of the traffic on that particular track, if possible.

At all times when walking track, take note of and be prepared to use the spaces available for safety, clear of passing trains. Be careful to avoid those positions where clearance is insufficient.

Employees are particularly cautioned with respect to sections of track on which regular operation of passenger trains may at times be abandoned and which are used as lay-up tracks. Such tracks are likely to be used at any and irregular times by special trains such as work trains, lay-up trains, etc. At no time can any section of track be assumed to be definitely out of service, and employees must observe, when on or near tracks, the usual precautions regardless of any assumption as to operating schedules.

1. Safety rules are MOST useful because they

   A. make it unnecessary to think
   B. prevent carelessness
   C. are a guide to avoid common dangers
   D. make the workman responsible for any accident

1._____

2. A trackman walking a section of track should walk

   A. to the left of the tracks
   B. to the right of the tracks
   C. in the direction of traffic
   D. opposite to the direction of traffic

2._____

3. One precaution a trackman should ALWAYS take is to

   A. have power turned off on those tracks where he is walking
   B. place a red lantern behind him when walking back
   C. wave his lantern constantly when walking track
   D. note nearby safety spaces

3._____

4. Special trains are GENERALLY

   A. passenger trains on regular schedule
   B. express trains on local tracks
   C. work trains or lay-up trains
   D. trains going opposite to traffic

5. A trackman walking track should

   A. stay clear of all safety spaces
   B. expect all trains to be on schedule
   C. avoid tracks used by passenger trains
   D. carry a hand lantern

6. On sections of track not used for regular passenger trains, a trackman should

   A. follow the rules governing tracks in passenger train operation
   B. assume that no trains will be operating
   C. walk in the direction of traffic
   D. disregard the usual precautions

7. Safety spaces are provided in the subway for

   A. lay-up trains   B. passing trains
   C. employee's use   D. easier walking

8. A trackman would NOT expect lay-up tracks to be used by

   A. special trains
   B. trains carrying passengers
   C. work trains
   D. lay-up trains

Questions 9-17.

DIRECTIONS: Questions 9 through 17 are to be answered on the basis of the porters' instructions given below. Read these instructions carefully before answering these questions

PORTERS' INSTRUCTIONS

Railroad porters are prohibited from entering the token booths except for cleaning or relieving the railroad clerk. When the cleaning or relief has been completed, porters must leave booths immediately and must not loiter in or around the booths. Porters must not leave their equipment or supplies, such as dust pans, brooms, soap, etc., on any stairway, passageway, walkway, or in any place which may result in a hazard to passengers or others. Whenever an accident occurs on the station where the porter is assigned, he must submit a report on the prescribed form, always giving the condition of the place where the accident occurred. Porters must be in prescribed uniforms ready for work when reporting *on* and *off* duty.

9. The instructions would indicate that the porters' PRINCIPAL duty is to   9._____

   A. make out accident reports
   B. wear a uniform
   C. relieve the railroad clerk
   D. keep the station clean

10. Porters are permitted to enter token booths   10._____

    A. any time they wish
    B. after finishing cleaning
    C. to relieve the railroad clerk
    D. to avoid loitering elsewhere

11. The PROBABLE reason why porters cannot stay in the token booth even if their regular work is done is because   11._____

    A. they have a regular porters' room
    B. they are not trusted
    C. there is no room
    D. passengers may complain

12. Porters are used to relieve railroad clerks MAINLY because   12._____

    A. they need the training
    B. they are conveniently available
    C. their regular work is hard
    D. their work is similar

13. In submitting a report on an accident, the porter is instructed to   13._____

    A. explain the cause
    B. use any convenient paper
    C. give the condition of the place
    D. telephone it to his superior

14. The MOST likely reason for having special uniforms for porters is to   14._____

    A. give them authority
    B. avoid a variety of unpresentable clothes
    C. save them money
    D. permit them to enter without paying fare

15. Evidently, porters must be careful where they leave their equipment or supplies to avoid   15._____

    A. spoilage   B. theft
    C. loss of time   D. injury to passengers

16. Such instructions to porters are NECESSARY because   16._____

    A. there is no other way to do the work
    B. it creates respect for authority
    C. it avoids misunderstandings
    D. they are not expected to think

17. A porter need NOT be in uniform when

    A. doing dirty work
    B. on his day off
    C. reporting *off* duty
    D. relieving the railroad clerk

Questions 18-25.

DIRECTIONS: Questions 18 through 25 are to be answered on the basis of the information contained in the safety rules given below. Read these rules carefully before answering these questions.

TRACKMEN SAFETY RULES ON EMERGENCY ALARM SYSTEM

In case of an emergency requiring the removal of high voltage power from the contact rail, any trackman seeing such emergency shall immediately operate the nearest emergency alarm box, and then immediately use the emergency telephone alongside the box to notify the trainmaster of the nature of the trouble. High voltage will be turned on again only by telephone order from an employee specifically having such authority. The location of this equipment along the trackway is indicated by a blue light. Trackmen are required to know the location of such boxes and the procedure to follow in order to have high voltage contact rail power removed on sections of elevated structure trackway which may not be equipped with emergency alarm boxes.

18. The location of an emergency alarm box is indicated by a(n) _____ light.

    A. red   B. orange   C. green   D. blue

19. Operating an emergency alarm box

    A. calls the fire department
    B. removes power
    C. lights a blue light
    D. restores power

20. All trackmen

    A. have the authority to have power restored
    B. should know the location of emergency alarm boxes
    C. must call the trainmaster before operating an emergency alarm box
    D. do not have the right to operate an emergency alarm box

21. On a track having trains in operation, a nearby emergency alarm box would PROBABLY be operated if

    A. an employee cuts his hand
    B. the emergency telephone rings
    C. the blue light goes on
    D. a break is found in a running track rail

22. After operating an emergency alarm box, the trackman should use the emergency telephone immediately to speak to   22.____

    A. his supervisor
    B. the trainmaster
    C. the station agent
    D. his co-workers

23. It would be MOST important to have power restored as quickly as possible in order to reduce   23.____

    A. power waste
    B. train damage
    C. train delays
    D. fire hazard

24. If there are no emergency alarm boxes along a trackway, trackmen   24.____

    A. cannot have power shut off
    B. are not required to act in an emergency
    C. can have power shut off by following the proper procedure
    D. are forbidden to use the emergency telephone

25. On elevated structure trackways,   25.____

    A. emergency alarm boxes may not be found
    B. train delays never occur
    C. the trainmaster is not notified on power removal
    D. power is never removed

KEY (CORRECT ANSWERS)

1. C   11. A
2. D   12. B
3. D   13. C
4. C   14. B
5. D   15. D

6. A   16. C
7. C   17. B
8. B   18. D
9. D   19. B
10. C 20. B

21. D
22. B
23. C
24. C
25. A

TEST 3

DIRECTIONS: Each question or incomplete statement is followed by several suggested answers or completions. Select the one that BEST answers the question or completes the statement. *PRINT THE LETTER OF THE CORRECT ANSWER IN THE SPACE AT THE RIGHT.*

Questions 1-5.

DIRECTIONS: Questions 1 through 5 are to be answered on the basis of the paragraphs shown below covering the supply duties of assistant station supervisors. Refer to these paragraphs when answering these questions.

SUPPLY DUTIES OF ASSISTANT STATION SUPERVISORS

The assistant station supervisors on the 8 A.M. to 4 P.M. tour will be responsible for the ordering of porter cleaning supplies and will inventory individual stations under their jurisdiction in order to maintain the necessary supplies to insure proper sanitary standards. They will be responsible not only for the ordering of such supplies but will see to it that ordered supplies are distributed as required in accordance with order supply sheets. Assistant station supervisors on the 4 P.M. to 12 Midnight and 12 Midnight to 8 A.M. shift will cooperate with the A.M. station supervisor to properly control supplies.

The 4 P.M. to 12 Midnight assistant station supervisors will be responsible for the ordering and control of all stationery supplies used by railroad clerks in the performance of their duties. They will also see that supplies are kept in a neat and orderly manner. The assistant station supervisors in charge of *Supply Storerooms* will see to it that material so ordered will be given to the porters for delivery to the respective booths. Cooperation of all supervision applies in this instance.

The 12 Midnight to 8 A.M. assistant station supervisors will be responsible for the storing of materials delivered by special work train (sawdust, etc.). They will also see that all revenue bags which are torn, dirty, etc. are picked up and sent to the field office for delivery to the bag room.

Any supplies needed other than those distributed on regular supply days will be requested by submitting a requisition to the supply control desk for emergency delivery.

1. The assistant station supervisors who are responsible for ordering all stationery supplies used by railroad clerks are the ones on the _____ tour.   1.____

   A. 8 A.M. to 4 P.M.
   B. 4 P.M. to 12 Midnight
   C. 12 Midnight to 8 A.M.
   D. 4 P.M. to 2 P.M.

2. Storing of materials delivered by special work trains is the responsibility of assistant station supervisors on the _____ tour.   2.____

   A. 8 A.M. to 4 P.M.
   B. 4 P.M. to 12 Midnight
   C. 12 Midnight to 8 A.M.
   D. 4 P.M. to 2 P.M.

3. Torn revenue bags should be picked up and sent FIRST to

   A. the bag room
   B. the supply control desk
   C. a supply storeroom
   D. the field office

4. To obtain an emergency delivery of supplies on a day other than a regular supply day, a requisition should be submitted to the

   A. appropriate zone office
   B. appropriate field office
   C. supply control desk
   D. station supervisor

5. The assistant station supervisor responsible for ordering porter cleaning supplies will inventory individual stations PRIMARILY for the end purpose of

   A. insuring proper sanitary standards
   B. maintaining necessary supplies
   C. keeping track of supplies
   D. distributing supplies fairly

Questions 6-10.

DIRECTIONS: Questions 6 through 10 are to be answered on the basis of the paragraphs shown below entitled POSTING OF DIVERSION OF SERVICE NOTICES. Refer to these paragraphs when answering these questions.

POSTING OF DIVERSION OF SERVICE NOTICES

The following procedures concerning the receiving and posting of service diversion notices will be strictly adhered to:

Assistant station supervisors who receive notices will sign a receipt and return it to the Station Department Office. It will be their responsibility to ensure that all notices are posted at affected stations and a notation made in the transmittal logs. All excess notices will be tied and a notation made thereon, indicating the stations and the date notices were posted, and the name and pass number of the assistant station supervisor posting same. The word *EXCESS* is to be boldly written on bundled notices and the bundle placed in a conspicuous location. When loose notices, without any notations, are discovered in any field office, assistant station supervisor's office, or other Station Department locations, the matter is to be thoroughly investigated to make sure proper distribution has been completed. All stations where a diversion of service exists must be contacted daily by the assistant station supervisor covering that group and hour to ensure that a sufficient number of notices are posted and employees are aware of the situation. In any of the above circumstances, notation is to be made in the supervisory log. Station supervisors will be responsible for making certain all affected stations in their respective groups have notices posted and for making spot checks each day diversions are in effect.

6. An assistant station supervisor who has signed a receipt upon receiving service diversion notices must return the

   A. notice to the Station Department office
   B. receipt to the Station Department office
   C. receipt and the transmittal log to the affected stations
   D. transmittal log after making a notation in it

7. Of the following, the information which is NOT required to be written on a bundle of excess notices is the   7._____

   A. names of the stations where the notices were posted
   B. time of day when the notices were posted
   C. date when the notices were posted
   D. name and pass number of the assistant station supervisor posting the notices

8. If loose notices without notations on them are found, the situation should be investigated to make sure that the   8._____

   A. notices are properly returned to the Station Department
   B. assistant station supervisor responsible for the error is found
   C. notices are correct for the diversion involved
   D. notices have been distributed properly

9. To insure that employees are aware of a diversion in service, an assistant station supervisor covering the group and hour when a diversion exists must contact the involved stations   9._____

   A. immediately after the diversion
   B. on an hourly basis
   C. on a daily basis
   D. as often as possible

10. To make certain affected stations have notices posted when diversions occur, spot checks should be made by   10._____

    A. station supervisors daily
    B. station supervisors when necessary
    C. assistant station supervisors daily
    D. assistant station supervisors when necessary

Questions 11-15.

DIRECTIONS: Questions 11 through 15 are to be answered on the basis of the following paragraph entitled PROCEDURE FOR FLAGGING DISABLED TRAIN.

PROCEDURE FOR FLAGGING DISABLED TRAIN

If at any time it becomes necessary to operate a train from other than the forward cab of the leading car, a qualified Rapid Transit Transportation Department employee must be stationed on the forward end. The motorman and the aforesaid qualified employee must have a clear understanding as to the signals to be used between them as well as to the method of operation. They must know, by actual test, that they have communication between them. Flagging signals should be given at short intervals while train is in motion. If train is carrying passengers, they must be discharged at the next station. Motormen operating from other than the forward cab of the leading car must not advance the controller beyond the *series position*.

11. The qualified employee stationed at the forward end must NOT be a   11._____

    A. motorman   B. conductor
    C. motorman instructor D. road car inspector

12. While the train is in motion, the employees stationed at the forward end should give a   12.____
    flagging signal

    A. at frequent intervals
    B. every time the train is about to pass a fixed signal
    C. only when he wants the train speed changed
    D. only when he wants to check his understanding with the motorman

13. Motormen operating from other than the leading car must NOT advance the controller   13.____
    beyond

    A. switching   B. series   C. multiple   D. parallel

14. Considering the actual conditions on a passenger train in the subway, the MOST practi-   14.____
    cal method of communication between the motorman and the employee at the forward
    end would be by using the

    A. train public address system   B. buzzer signals
    C. whistle signals   D. lantern signals

15. The BEST reason for discharging passengers at the next station under these conditions   15.____
    is that

    A. carrying passengers would cause additional delays
    B. it is not possible to operate safely
    C. the motorman cannot see the station stop markers
    D. the four lights at the front of the train will be red

Questions 16-25.

DIRECTIONS: Questions 16 through 25, inclusive, are based on the description given in the following special assignment for a group of cleaners. Read the description carefully before answering these questions. Be sure to consider ONLY the information contained in these paragraphs.

SPECIAL ASSIGNMENT

A special assignment of washing the ceilings and the tile walls of a number of stations on a particular line was given to a group of railroad cleaners. The stations included in the assignment were both local and express stations, and the only means of transferring between the uptown and the downtown trains without going to the street was to be found at the express stations. The stations to be cleaned were 2nd Street, 9th Street, 16th Street, 22nd Street, 29th Street, 36th Street, 44th Street, 52nd Street, 60th Street, and 69th Street. Of these, the express stations were located at 16th Street, 44th Street, and 69th Street.

Only the uptown sides of the stations were to be cleaned, as another gang was to clean the downtown sides. The cleaning operations were to start at 2nd Street and progress uptown. The materials furnished to perform this work consisted of pails, soap, long-handled brushes, mops, rags, and canvas covers for scales and vending machines.

The instructions were to scrub a surface first with a brush that had been immersed in a pail of soapy water, and then follow up by brushing with clear water. Any equipment on stations that was left uncovered and was splashed in the cleaning process was to be wiped clean with a rag.

16. The total number of different kinds of materials furnished to do the work of the special assignment was 16._____

    A. 5　　　　　B. 6　　　　　C. 7　　　　　D. 8

17. Benches on station platforms were to be 17._____

    A. moved out of the work area
    B. covered with canvas
    C. wiped clean with a rag if splashed
    D. rinsed with clear water

18. Of the materials furnished, the instructions did NOT definitely call for the use of 18._____

    A. mops　　　B. brushes　　　C. pails　　　D. rags

19. The FIRST operation cleaners were instructed to do was to 19._____

    A. clean walls with scouring cleanser
    B. scrub ceilings with clear water
    C. wipe vending machines clean with rags
    D. scrub surfaces with soapy water

20. Furnished materials that were NOT used in the washing of ceilings included 20._____

    A. soap　　　B. pails　　　C. rags　　　D. water

21. Long-handled brushes were probably furnished because 21._____

    A. ladders cannot be used on stations
    B. such brushes are easier to handle than ordinary brushes
    C. a better job can be done, since both hands are used
    D. some areas could not be reached otherwise

22. Of the total number of stations included in the assignment, the number which were express stations was 22._____

    A. 3　　　　　B. 7　　　　　C. 10　　　　　D. 20

23. A cleaner working in the *uptown* gang at 52nd Street Station was sent by his supervisor to get some supplies from the *downtown* gang which happened to be working at the same station. 23._____
    The cleaner would have displayed good judgment if he

    A. boarded a downtown train to 44th Street, crossed over, and then boarded an uptown train
    B. descended to the tracks and crossed over cautiously
    C. boarded an uptown train to 69th Street, crossed over, and then boarded a downtown train
    D. went directly up to the street and crossed over

24. After finishing the assigned work at 44th Street, the men on this assignment were scheduled to go next to _____ Street. 24._____

    A. 16th B. 36th C. 52nd D. 69th

25. A passenger at 29th Street wishing to transfer from a downtown local to an uptown local without paying an additional fare should transfer at _____ Street. 25._____

    A. 44th B. 16th C. 36th D. 22nd

KEY (CORRECT ANSWERS)

1. B
2. C
3. D
4. C
5. A

6. B
7. B
8. D
9. C
10. A

11. D
12. A
13. B
14. B
15. A

16. B
17. C
18. A
19. D
20. C

21. D
22. A
23. D
24. C
25. B